Disclaimer

Air Fryer Cookbook

200 Fast, Easy and Delicious Air Fryer Recipes

By Susan Hollister
Copyright © 2018

Table of Contents

CHAPTER 5: MOUTHWATERING CHICKEN AND TURKEY RECIPES 98

CHAPTER 6: SEAFOOD FIT FOR ROYALTY

CHAPTER 7: BEEF MEALS THAT EVERYONE LOVES..151

CHAPTER 10: AMAZING SIDE DISHES..... 218

CHAPTER 11: DESSERTS, SWEETS AND OTHER TREATS......................237

CHAPTER 12 : YOUR FAVORITE FROZEN FOODS MADE EASY..........................268

Introduction

Congratulations, you have made a great decision in purchasing this Air Fryer cookbook! Included are 200 delicious Air Fryer recipes that everyone is sure to love! In the following pages you will also discover all the different ways to make tasty foods in your Air Fryer. Not only will these foods be delicious, but they will contain fewer calories and be healthier for you! The recipes are easy to make and easy to follow. You will also absolutely love how quick and effortless it is to cook with an Air fryer. You will find that the recipes in this book taste fresh, crispy and delicious!

Air Fryers enable you to create incredible meals by frying with air. These appliances allow you to cook normally deep fried foods with 80% less oil while also making the food healthier to eat. It uses super-heated air to cook the food and it has a fan that distributes the air much like a convection oven.

Not only can you make foods you would normally deep fry, but you can make other recipes in less time that it takes in your oven. Make roast beef, ham, lamb chops, hamburgers, scrambled eggs, quiche, baked apples, cakes, pies and cookies. With a few accessories you can make just about anything you can make in your oven in a fraction of the time. Fried chicken and other favorites come out crisp and moist and you won't need a napkin to wipe the grease off your fingers.

Your Air Fryer will help you to avoid grease and still be able to eat the foods you love like French fries, country fried steak and all sorts of great fish dishes. Not only that, but you can make other recipes like roast beef, rack of lamb, pulled pork, lobster tails and many more main dish entrees. When you are done with those, make delicious appetizers like stuffed mushrooms, potato skins and onion rings. I have also included some sweet treats like chocolate cake, apple pie, cookies and more all made in the Air Fryer.

This book does not stop there. Not many frozen foods come with directions on how to cook them in an air fryer. I have included easy directions to follow for cooking all sorts of your favorite frozen foods. You will find that your frozen food comes out with less grease, crispy and delicious. Make frozen chicken nuggets, poppers, pizza rolls, hamburgers, chicken breasts and more in a fraction of the time it normally takes to make them other ways.

With an air fryer it takes less time to cook and you can cook just about anything! Your meals will have less calories and less cholesterol than traditional recipes. Cooking with an Air Fryer is a win win situation and this book will tell you how to create delicious meals quickly and easily. Included are breakfast, lunch and dinner recipes. There are also delicious appetizers, snacks, side dishes and sweet desert recipes.

Keep on reading to learn everything you need to know about using an Air Fryer to create delicious meals with less grease and more flavor!

Chapter 1: All You Need To Know About The Air Fryer

The technology used in air fryers is called "rapid air Technology" and it causes the heat to be pushed by a rapidly turning fan. Ovens, unless they are convection ovens, do not have fans that constantly circulate the heat. Air fryers have a removable basket in which the food sits and the hot air circulates all around to cook the food.

One of the most popular things to make in an air fryer is French fries. These tasty treats are normally submerged in a vat full of oil and are dep fried at a high heat. The potatoes soak up quite a bit of the oil and retain it and it is consumed. We all know that oil is not necessarily good for the body. Some oils cause plaque to form in our blood vessels and encumber our bodies with extra fat. If you reduce the amount of oil and the food tastes great and sometimes better, how can you go wrong? I use my air fryer almost every week to make sweet potato fries. I just peel the potato, chop it into thick strips, toss them in 1 tablespoon olive oil and some seasoning and fry them up in the air fryer. They come out crisp on the outside and tender inside and are better than any fries made in hot oil and it only takes about 10 minutes to make and cook them.

What Can You Cook In An Air Fryer?

You can cook anything you would normally deep fry, but that isn't all. Fries, chicken nuggets, fried chicken, fried fish and all those other unhealthy foods cook up great in an air fryer and are safer to eat. But that is not all you can do in an air fryer. I make scrambled eggs for breakfast or French Toast. I can cook up empanadas or Chinese dumplings for my lunch. It isn't hard to make meatloaf, pork chops, salmon, country fried steak or BBQ chicken in the air fryer. As long as the dish isn't liquid, like soup or stew, it is a possibility in an air fryer. It is also possible to make cake, hand pies and other desserts in the air fryer.

The basket of the air fryer has little slits in it so that the air can flow through. Some things I make in my air fryer are not suitable to put in that basket because it would leak all over. To remedy that, I use a small 6 to 4-inch metal cake pan, ceramic ramekins or small metal bowl with a flat bottom to put things in too cook, like my scrambled eggs. Some air fryers even come with an accessory like this to put in the basket. This makes so many more possibilities when it comes to items you can make in an air fryer.

Is Food Really Healthier When Made In An Air Fryer?

The fan in the air fryer not only circulates hot air around the food, but it also circulates out droplets of oil and creates a chemical reaction called The Mallard Effect. This effect causes the food to turn brown and crispy and adds some flavor to the food. Air fried foods contain much less fat, but they taste is about the same or better. Fried chicken made in an air fryer contains about the same amount of fat as a roasted or baked chicken. Not only do foods contain less fat, they also have fewer calories. When food is fried a compound is created on the food that we consume. This substance is acrylamide and it is thought to be a carcinogen (causes cancer). A study was performed and it was found that the acrylamide content was reduced by 90% when food was cooked in an air fryer. I have an issue with fried foods. I eat them and that results in terrible heart burn and stomachs. I can eat fries and other fried foods in the air fryer with no effect. I can say with certainty because of my own weight loss that foods made in an air fryer are healthier for me.

Benefits

The pros vastly outweigh the cons of having an air fryer, in my opinion. I use mine all the time and I have noticed a reduction in my gas bill (I have a gas stove) and no noticeable increase in my electric bill. That is a definite plus for me.

Benefits
- Food is healthier because oil use is greatly reduced. Still, everything comes out crispy and brown that is supposed to.
- Food cooks quicker. Heat does not escape from the air fryer like it does on a cooktop or oven. It takes less time to cook or reheat food because it stays in the air fryer and circulates.
- The air fryer is more efficient. Because the heat stays in the unit and does not vent, it cooks more efficiently and faster without using as much electricity. I hate turning my oven on in the summer because it heats up the house. Not so with an air fryer. heat created in the air fryer stays in the air fryer.
- It is versatile and you can make a variety of foods from breakfast all the way to dessert.
- Most units are small and fit on the counter top or in a cupboard for storage. That can also be a con if you don't like stuff sitting on your countertops.
- They clean rather easily and most parts, like the basket and what holds the basket, can be put in a dishwasher.
- Heating up frozen foods that would normally go in an oven at high temperature can be cooked in a matter of minutes including chicken tenders and nuggets, fish sticks and frozen fries.

Types of Air Fryers

Three types of Air Fryers are available on the market today and include:

- Halogen – that uses a halogen light bulb to cook. These often have a transparent glass cover so you can watch the whole cooking process without opening the air fryer.

- Dynamic – has a paddle that rotates the food while it is cooking so there is no need to turn it. This is nice when you are making fries, but not so good for other foods. If I put my empanadas or dumplings in one of these and the paddle rotates it, it would have stuffing all over the place.
- Static Air - is where everything stays still except the air inside heated by coil elements and circulated by a fan. This is what most people have when getting an air fryer.

Air fryers come in many different sizes. Mine cooks 1.8 pounds of food at a time and has a basket that is about 6-inches in diameter. Other types cook 1.5 and up to 2.5 pounds of food at a time.

Accessories

Some air fryers come with accessories and they include:
- Racks that go inside the basket
- Grill pan
- Baking dish
- Steamer
- Silicone pan or cups
- Rubber ended tongs that do not scratch

It is worth getting the silicone pan or cups, steamer and baking dish and necessary to get rubber ended tongs. Don't try removing food from the basket with a fork because you will scratch the surface of the basket and everything will stick in the future.

I found a few small round layer cake pan at my local second hand store. The 6-inch one fits perfectly into the air fryer with a little room to fit the rubber tipped tongs in to get it out.

The 4-inch one is perfect for making single serve omelets or you can use a ramekin.

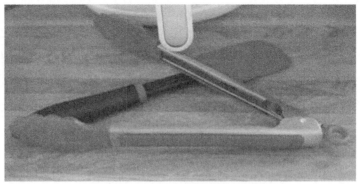

Accessories with Silicone Tips

Tips

The following tips will help you make the best of your air fryer:

- I suggest preheating your air fryer before putting anything in it. Not all recipes call for this, but I do it anyway. I set the fryer for the temperature stated in the recipe and cook the food 1 to 4 minutes. The bigger the item is that goes in, the longer I preheat. If I am cooking a few fries, I preheat 1 or 2 minutes and if I am cooking two chicken breasts, I would preheat 4 minutes. I also preheat a little longer if the food being placed in the air fryer is frozen. If I make my own chicken nuggets, I preheat 2 minutes. If I am doing frozen chicken nuggets, I preheat 4 minutes.

- Many recipes require cooking spray to be sprayed on the food, so make sure you have a variety including butter flavored and olive or canola oil types. I actually prefer a kitchen pump spray bottle that allows me to put olive oil and other oils in to spray.

- When breading items to be air fried, it is important to dredge in flour first and then press the breadcrumbs into the meat. The fan puts out a lot of power and will blow the breadcrumbs off if you don't do it right.

- Putting a tablespoon or so of water in the drawer that holds the basket will stop greasy foods like bacon or ham to not smoke.

- Secure tops of sandwiches with toothpicks and cut them down just above the food they are holding. The air fryer fan is very powerful and often lifts the top bread from a sandwich while cooking.

- Never overcrowd the basket because the food will not get done properly. Everything must be in a single layer and not overlapping.

- Flip most items cooked in the air fryer half way through the time allotted for cooking. This allows the food to cook evenly. Of course, there will be some things you can't do this with.

- Always check meat and other foods that could give you food poisoning with an instant-read thermometer to make sure it is really done. If it does not meet requirements for that food, put it back in and cook it a little longer (maybe 1 or 2 minutes) and check again. This is especially necessary when cooking frozen foods.

- If you use a light weight cake pan or metal bowl in your air fryer do not be concerned if it makes a lot of noise. The fan is going to push it around in there and you will hear it clanging especially if there isn't much in there. To make scrambled eggs you must air fry the butter in a pan while you are preheating the air fryer and it will clang around for the whole 2 minutes it is preheating. Once you put the eggs in, it weights it down and it will no longer move around or make noise.

Now it is time to get cooking with your air fryer. Remember to always check while cooking because all air fryers do not cook at the same temps and times. Start with breakfast and make your way to snacks, desserts and cooking readymade items.

Chapter 2: World Class Breakfast Recipes

There are many breakfast possibilities when it comes to making it in an air fryer. You can make donuts, eggs, hash browns, frittatas, quiches, French toast, sausage and more. The great thing about them is that you don't have to saturate anything in butter or oil for it to taste spectacular enough to make your taste buds stand at attention, even early in the morning. Give some of these recipes a try for breakfast or lunch or even dinner. There is even a muffin recipe in this bunch.

Air Fried Doughnut Holes

I remember my mom making doughnuts on Saturday mornings and she always liked to make holes because they were a little easier to make since you didn't have to roll out the dough and cut the doughnuts out with a cookie cutter. Just pat out the dough and pull off uniform pieces rolling them into little balls. They were bite sized and fun to eat. These doughnut holes are soft in the center and crispy on the outside. They melt in your mouth and the cinnamon and sugar coating makes them sweet. This recipe makes about 2 to 3 dozen doughnut holes depending on the size in which they are made. I make mine golf ball sized.

Ingredients:
2 ½ tablespoons butter, room temperature
½ cup granulated sugar
2 large egg yolks

2 ¼ cup all-purpose flour
1 ½ teaspoon baking powder
1 teaspoon salt
½ cup sour cream

Ingredients – Sugar Coating:
1/3 cup granulated sugar
1 teaspoon cinnamon
1 tablespoon melted butter

Directions:
1. Place the butter and sugar in a bowl and press to make a crumbly mixture. I use a pastry cutter or two table knives and that seems to do the trick.
2. Add the egg yolks and stir with a wooden spoon until they are completely combined.
3. In another bowl, combine the flour, baking powder and salt and whisk it up.
4. Put about 1/3 of the flour mixture in the sugar and egg mixture and ½ of the sour cream and mix well.
5. Mix in the rest of the flour mixture and sour cream.
6. Cover the bowl with plastic wrap and put it in the refrigerator for at least 30 minutes (can be overnight).
7. In a small bowl, whisk the cinnamon and sugar and set the bowl aside.
8. When ready to air fry, take the dough out of the refrigerator and pat flat on a flat surface.
9. Preheat the air fryer to 350 degrees for about to 4 minutes.
10. Break off uniform pieces of the dough and roll into balls placing them on wax paper. I put all my doughnut holes on wax paper because you can only do a few at a time. Brush the doughnut holes you will be cooking first with the melted butter.
11. Put as many can fit in the basket of the air fryer without piling them on top of each other and cook for 4 minutes, check to make sure they are not burning and shake to roll and cook another 3 to 4 minutes or until crispy.

12. Pour the doughnut holes out into a basket covered with paper towels and let cool slightly.
13. When they are safe to touch, roll them in the cinnamon and sugar and serve.

Air Fryer Breakfast Burrito

This is a filling breakfast entrée that takes only about 10 minutes to make. You do need a pan or tin that fits inside the air fryer basket. I have made it in the basket with nonstick spray and it comes out good but is very messy to clean. I like the flat surface instead of the bumpy basket surface on which to cook the eggs. This makes 1 serving.

Ingredients:
2 eggs
1 pinch salt
1 pinch pepper
1 flour tortilla
2 tablespoons salsa
3 or 4 slices of deli turkey breast
¼ of a red bell pepper, seeded and sliced
¼ avocado, sliced
1/8 cup shredded Mozzarella cheese

Directions:

1. Beat the eggs with the salt and pepper.
2. Pour the eggs in the nonstick pan that fits inside the air fryer or in the nonstick sprayed basket of the air fryer.
3. Set the temperature for 200 degrees F for 5 minutes.
4. Remove the pan and scrape out the egg onto a plate. The egg should be set and if not put it back in the air fryer for a few more minutes.
5. Spread the tortilla out on a flat surface and spread the salsa on top.
6. Cover the salsa with the turkey slices, put the egg on top and sprinkle with bell pepper and avocado. Sprinkle with the cheese and roll tight.
7. Place the burrito, seam side down in the basket of the air fryer and set for 180 degrees F cooking for 3 minutes or until the tortilla browns and the cheese is melted.

Air Fryer Perfect Omelet

A pan that fits inside the basket of the air fryer is needed for this recipe that makes a lovely omelet. Use a variety of vegetables, not just ones used in the recipe. These are just suggestions. I like to use green onions, chopped mushrooms and red bell peppers, but broccoli, spinach or cauliflower works well too. I also enjoy the flavor of Herbs de Province in this dish but some people do not like the taste of lavender in food. If you are one of them, use Italian seasoning instead. This recipe makes 1 omelet.

Ingredients:

2 eggs

¼ cup milk

1 pinch of salt

1 teaspoon Herbs de Province

2 tablespoons chopped cooked ham or bacon

2 tablespoons chopped green onion

2 tablespoons chopped red bell pepper

2 tablespoons chopped mushrooms

¼ cup shredded Mozzarella or Swiss cheese

Directions:

1. Whisk the eggs, milk, salt and Herbs de Province in a bowl.
2. Mix in the ham or bacon, green onion, red bell pepper and mushrooms.
3. Pour the mixture into a nonstick sprayed pan that fits into the air fryer.
4. Set for 350 degrees F and set for 4 minutes.
5. Open the air fryer and sprinkle the cheese on top of the omelet. Cook another 4 to 5 minutes or until the eggs are set.
6. Use a rubber spatula to loosen the omelet from the pan and place it on a plate to serve.

Breakfast Hash Browns

This recipe makes a flavorful breakfast all on its own. You don't need a pile of eggs or anything else with it. A frying pan on the stove is used for some of the ingredients and the mixture needs to be in the refrigerator about 20 minutes. I get mine ready the night before and cook it for breakfast. The recipe makes 8 servings of hash browns. Serve with ketchup or BBQ sauce.

Ingredients:
4 large white potatoes, peeled and grated
2 teaspoons vegetable oil, divided
2 tablespoons corn meal
½ teaspoon salt
½ teaspoon pepper
1 teaspoon garlic powder
1 teaspoon onion powder
2 teaspoons pepper flakes, crushed

Directions:
1. Soak the shredded potatoes in enough cold water to cover them for 15 minutes. Drain, soak again another 15 minutes and drain. Pat dry with a paper towel.
2. Heat 1 teaspoon of the vegetable oil in a frying pan over medium heat and pour in the shredded potatoes. Sauté for about 3 to 4 minutes and let cool.
3. Add the corn meal, salt, pepper, garlic powder, onion powder and pepper flakes to the potatoes and mix well.
4. Use your hands to spread the mixture in the bottom of a 9-inch deep dish pie plate. cover with plastic wrap and refrigerate 20 minutes or overnight.
5. Preheat the air fryer to 350 degrees F and cut the hash browns in 8 wedges.
6. Brush the basket of the air fryer with the remaining 1 teaspoon of oil and put 4 of the wedges in.
7. Fry 15 minutes, flip with a plastic spatula and fry 6 more minutes. Remove and do the same with the other 4 wedges.
8. Serve hot.

Breakfast in a Muffin Cup

Make this breakfast entrée in muffin cups. You can use paper cups, but they do tend to smolder and smoke a bit. I prefer using silicon cupcake liners. The recipe uses egg substitute and makes it cholesterol friendly. This makes 6 cups. I cannot fit 6 of them in my air fryer so I must do it in batches of three.

Ingredients:
6 tablespoons cooked and crumbled sausage patty
6 tablespoons frozen chopped spinach, thawed and as dry as possible
6 tablespoons shredded Co-Jack cheese
¼ cup egg substitute
salt and pepper to taste

Directions:
1. Cook the sausage on the stove, drain and let cool. Crumble when cool and set aside.
2. Thaw the spinach, drain and squeeze it dry in paper towels to make it as dry as possible and set aside.
3. Take 6 muffin cups and place three in the basket of the air fryer.
4. Place 1 tablespoon of the sausage and 1 tablespoon of the spinach in the bottom of each muffin cup.
5. Sprinkle each cup with some cheese reserving enough for the other 3 cups.

6. Divide the egg substitute between the three cups reserving enough for the other 3 cups.
7. Sprinkle salt and pepper over each of the three cups in the air fryer.
8. Set the temperature for 350 degrees F and bake for 10 minutes. Check three times during the cooking to make sure they aren't burning, especially if using paper muffin cups.
9. Carefully remove from the air fryer and continue with the other three muffin cups in the same manner.
10. Serve hot.

Breakfast Sausage Wraps

These little gems are easy to make and both kids and adults love them. They are sort of like the old recipe you had as a kid for pigs in a blanket where mom took a hot dog, slit it open and put a strip of cheese in and then rolled it in a tubed or canned crescent roll and baked them. Cook in batches of 4 and serve with dipping sauce of ketchup or BBQ sauce. I like them for lunch too. This makes 8 wraps.

Ingredients:
8 pre-cooked sausages (look like hot dogs0
8 thin strip slices of your preferred cheese (I like cheddar but you can go with smoky gouda, or hot pepper cheese if you are brave)
1 can – 8 count refrigerated canned crescent rolls

Directions:

1. Cut the sausage long ways down the length but not all the way through.
2. Insert the cheese strip in the cut.
3. Unfold the crescent roll dough and separate.
4. Place the stuffed sausage at the wide end of the dough and roll to the pointy end. Tuck in ends and pinch dough shut. Continue until all sausages are covered with dough.
5. Place four in the bottom of a nonstick sprayed air fryer basket and bake at 380 degrees F for 3 minutes. Check to see if they are brown and hot and if not, put them in a few more minutes.
6. When done, let them cook for a minute or two and remove with tongs. Continue with the other four wraps.
7. Serve hot.

Broccoli Cheese Quiche

They say real men don't eat quiche but they will if it tastes as good as this one does. The cheesy flavor is very good and it is all done in an air fryer in about 25 to 30 minutes and makes 2 servings. Chop your vegetables the night before and all you must do is whisk the eggs and cook in the morning. You do need a dish or pan that fits inside the air fryer and I use a 4-inch round cake pan.

Ingredients:
3 large carrots

28

1 medium head of broccoli
1 tomato, sliced
1 teaspoon dried thyme
1 teaspoon dried parsley
salt and pepper to taste
2 large eggs
½ cup grated cheddar cheese
1 ½ tablespoon Feta cheese
¾ cup whole milk

Directions:

1. Peel and dice the carrots and cut the broccoli in florets. Place in a steamer (I use my instant pot but a metal or bamboo steamer over boiling water works well) and steam until the vegetables are somewhat soft but not mushy. Pour them in a colander and let them drain before putting them away for morning or using.
2. Slice the tomato in thin slices and set aside. (You can do this the night before and save in the refrigerator too).
3. In a bowl, combine the thyme, parsley, salt and pepper. Add the eggs and milk and whisk it all together.
4. Take your vegetable mixture and place it on the bottom of a nonstick sprayed baking pan that fits into the air fryer basket. Layer on the sliced tomatoes and sprinkle half of the cheddar and half of the feta over top.
5. Slowly pour the egg mixture over top.
6. Sprinkle with the remaining feta and cheddar and place in the air fryer basket.
7. Bake 350 degrees F for 20 minutes checking for doneness after about 15 minutes. If the quiche jiggles too much after 20, put it in for about 4 to 5 more minutes until more firm. It will firm up more when it cools.

Canned Biscuit Doughnuts

Use grand sized biscuits in a can to make 8 big doughnuts and 8 doughnut holes that are spicy and sweet. They are dipped in sugar cinnamon, ginger and allspice for a taste of fall and they are so easy to make it will astound you.

Ingredients:

4 tablespoons dark brown sugar
½ to 1 teaspoon cinnamon (more if you like cinnamon)
1/8 teaspoons ginger
1 pinch of allspice
1/3 cup granulated sugar
1 can Grands Flakey biscuits in a can (8 of them)
3 tablespoons melted butter

Directions:

1. In a small bowl, combine the brown sugar, cinnamon, ginger, allspice and granulated sugar. Whisk well and set the bowl aside for later.
2. Remove the biscuits from the can and set on a flat cutting board. Do not flatten them but cut a 1-inch circle out of the center.
3. Put 4 doughnuts in the basket of the air fryer and set for 350 degrees and cook for 5 minutes. They should be puffy and brown, if not, give them a few more minutes. Remove from the air fryer and put the other four in and fry.
4. Fry the doughnut holes 3 minutes.
5. After removing them from the air fryer, brush with the melted butter and drop in the sugar and spice mixture pressing it in

the doughnuts on both sides and rolling the doughnut holes in it.
6. Shake off the excess sugar and serve.

Cranberry Pecan Air Fryer Muffins

These muffins do not contain refined sugar and no dairy or gluten. Instead cashew milk, date sugar and almond flour are used. I use fresh cranberries that sort of pop and flood your mouth with flavor. The recipe makes 6 to 8 muffins. Everything is combined in a blender. I use a jar blender, but you can use a regular one too. I use the silicone cupcake or muffin liners mainly because they are safer than using paper ones.

Ingredients:
2 large eggs
½ teaspoon vanilla
¼ cup cashew milk
¼ cup date sugar
1 teaspoon baking powder
1 ½ cups almond flour
¼ teaspoon cinnamon
1/8 teaspoon salt
½ cup fresh cranberries, divided
¼ cup chopped pecans, divided

Directions:
1. Crack the eggs in a blender container and add the milk and vanilla. Blend for 20 to 30 seconds.

31

2. Add the date sugar, baking powder, almond flour, cinnamon and salt and blend.
3. If using a jar blender, remove the container from the blender and stir in ½ the cranberries and ½ the pecans. If using a regular blender, scrape into a bowl and stir in the cranberries and pecans.
4. Distribute evenly between the 6 to 8 muffin cups. Top each muffin with the rest of the cranberries and pecans evenly.
5. Place 3 to 4 muffins in the basket of the air fryer and bake at 325 degrees F for 12 to 15 minutes. Insert a toothpick in one of the muffins and if it comes out clean, they are done. If not, put them back in for a few minutes and check again.
6. Remove the muffins with tongs and let cool while the next batch bakes.

Crispy, Delicious Bacon Cooked in An Air Fryer

You can make bacon in the air fryer and it comes out less greasy. Do as much as you want but only put as much bacon that will make a single layer in the bottom of the basket.

Ingredients:
Bacon (I can fit about 5 to 6 strips in mine)
2 tablespoons water

Directions:
1. Set the air fryer for 350 degrees F and preheat for 2 minutes.

2. Place bacon in bottom of basket of air fryer.
3. Add water to the basket as this will prevent smoking.
4. Cook the bacon 8 to 10 minutes, check for crispness, flip the strips and cook another 2 minutes.
5. Always drain the basket of grease between batches.

Eggs Benedict In An Air Fryer

Small ceramic ramekins are needed to make this dish. Depending on the size you can fit in 2 at a time and this recipe makes 4, so two batches are necessary. I use Canadian bacon that looks more like a ham slice when I can find it. The bacon is good but doesn't taste as nice. I have a problem with making Hollandaise sauce, but I rarely have a problem with this one.

Ingredients:
4 piece Canadian Bacon or bacon, precooked
4 eggs
salt and pepper to taste
2 English Muffins
3 egg yolks
5 tablespoons butter, melted
1 tablespoons lemon juice

Directions:
1 Preheat the air fryer to 320 degrees F for 4 minutes.
2 Place your Canadian bacon or regular bacon in a skillet over medium heat and fry. Once done set it aside for later.

3 Spray each ramekin with nonstick spray and crack an egg in each one. Season with salt and pepper.
4 Carefully place 2 of the ramekins in and cook for 3 minutes.
5 Check doneness of the egg and if not done put in another 2 minutes.
6 Carefully remove the ramekins and set aside. Halve the English muffins and put a top and bottom in the air fryer. Set for 365 degrees F and cook 3 minutes. This should toast it. Remove it from the air fryer.
7 Do the same with the other 2 ramekins and other English muffin.
8 While everything is cooking, combine in a blender, the egg yolks, butter and lemon juice. Combine until frothy. Pour into a sauce pan and whisk while heating. Once it starts bubbling around the edges and is steaming, it should thicken a little and is ready.
9 To assemble, place 1 half of an English muffin on a plate and top with the Canadian or regular bacon. Run a knife around the edge of the ramekin and use a rubber spatula to get the egg out and place on top.
10 Spoon over the Hollandaise sauce and serve.

Fancy Soufflé

Ramekins are needed for this recipe too. Spray them with nonstick butter flavored spray before filling. This is one you cannot open and close the door of the air fryer often for because it will make the soufflé fall. It might burn the first time, it might be soggy the second time but by the third time you try you should know how your air fryer works and put it in for the right amount of time.

Ingredients:
4 eggs
1 teaspoon dry parsley
1 pinch red pepper flakes
4 tablespoons light cream

Directions:
1. Use a 4 cup glass measuring cup and crack the four eggs into it.
2. Add the parsley and red pepper flakes and whisk.

3. Whisk in the light cream until it is thoroughly whisked together.
4. Spray 4 ramekins with nonstick spray.
5. Fill each ramekin half way with the egg mixture and place two of them in the air fryer.
6. Set for 390 degrees F and bake 5 minutes. This will create a soft soufflé. If you want it a litter firmer, go for 8 minutes.
7. Let cool a minute and lift out with tongs. Place the other two ramekins in and repeat.

Fried Low Carb Frittata

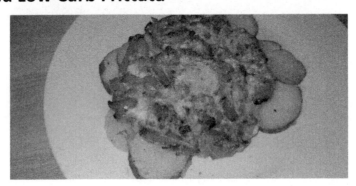

This is a versatile recipe because you can use whatever you want in your frittata. You will need a baking pan like a 4-inch cake pan or mini loaf pan that fits inside the basket of the air fryer. The recipe asks for sausage, but you can also use a few strips of bacon, a slice of chopped ham or some shredded chicken. When it comes to the bell pepper in the recipe, you can also either substitute or add mushrooms, spinach, broccoli or tomatoes, just do not go over 1 ½ tablespoons of all combined. The recipe asks for shredded cheddar, but I like shredded Swiss better. Shred whatever hard cheese you have and use it. This recipe makes 1 individual frittata.

Ingredients:
1 tablespoon melted butter
1 sausage patty, chopped
2 large eggs
1/8 teaspoon salt

1 pinch ground black pepper
1 teaspoon green onion, chopped
1 tablespoon bell pepper, chopped
2 tablespoons shredded cheddar

Directions:
1. Brush the melted butter on the bottom and up the sides of the pan. There should be enough to leave a little pool in the bottom.
2. Add the sausage and air fry at 350 degrees F for 5 minutes.
3. While the sausage is frying, break the eggs in a bowl and add season with salt and pepper. Whisk well.
4. Add the green onion and bell pepper to the eggs and whisk.
5. Once the sausage is done cooking, pour in the egg mixture and sprinkle with cheese.
6. Turn on the air fryer at 350 degrees F for another 5 minutes.

Homemade Toaster Fruit Tarts

This recipe takes toaster tarts to a new level. They are made with refrigerated pie crust and jam. I have used low sugar jam and they came out grate. Use any flavor jam you like but I particularly like strawberry or raspberry. Peach tastes good too and no one in my house really liked the grape, but someone in yours might. Leave them plain or make a powder sugar and milk glaze and sprinkles to put on top. I have included a low sugar glaze made with cream cheese that works well too. This makes 6 tarts but make them in two batches of three. They must cool before you remove them from the basket or they will crack, so I refrigerate the others on a plate covered with plastic wrap and do them the next day.

Ingredients:

2 refrigerated pie crusts
1/3 cup strawberry, raspberry or other fruit jam
1 teaspoon cornstarch
Ingredients For the Cream Cheese Frosting:
1 ounce reduced fat cream cheese, softened
½ cup plain, non-fat vanilla Greek yogurt
1 teaspoon Stevia

Directions:

1. Unfold one of the pie crusts on a flat surface covered with wax paper. Push them out into a squarish shape instead of round and cut into 3 long rectangles. Do the same with the other pie crust.
2. In a bowl, mix the jam with the cornstarch. Divide this between the six rectangles. Place the jam in the upper top third of each rectangle and spread out a little with a butter knife. Bring the bottom up over the jam and match the ends and press down on the edges.
3. Crimp all the edges of the tart by pressing with the tines of a fork dipped in water. Poke a few holes in the top of each tart with the fork so steam can escape.
4. Place 2 or three tarts, however many will fit without overlapping) in the bottom of the basket of the air fryer. Spray with butter flavor nonstick spray.
5. Set for 380 degrees F for 10 minutes. Put on pause at 5 minutes and take a look to make sure they aren't getting too brown. If they are already brown at 5 minutes adjust time down to about 8 minutes total.
6. When done, remove basket from air fryer and set on heat resistant surface. Let the tarts cool before you move them out or they will break.
7. To make the topping, mix the softened cream cheese, yogurt and Stevia in a bowl.

8. Once the tarts are out of the air fryer, spread on top.

Kid Friendly French Toast Sticks

Serve French Toast Sticks with Syrup, Jam Or A Sprinkle Of Cinnamon And Sugar

Kids don't like a bunch of flavors mixed together so keep it simple with a little cinnamon, sugar and vanilla. However, adults may enjoy a bit more spice on their French toast so add 1/8 teaspoon nutmeg, 1 pinch of ground cloves and 1 pinch of allspice to the mix. It is possible to use either wheat or white sandwich bread, but the sticks tend to break from the weight of the egg dip. When making sticks, I use a day old French or Italian bread cut thick. For adults, you do not have to cut the bread in sticks. Just leave it whole and do one slice at a time. I serve these with maple syrup, but also with jam on occasion. This recipe will serve 2 people.

Ingredients:
2 eggs, beaten
1 pinch salt
¼ teaspoon cinnamon
½ teaspoon sugar
½ teaspoon vanilla
4 slices bread
2 to 3 tablespoons soft, spreadable butter

Directions:
1. Preheat the air fryer to 390 degrees F for 4 minutes.

2. Beat the eggs in a bowl and add the salt, cinnamon, sugar and vanilla. Whisk well. The cinnamon tends to float to the top so you might have to keep whisking after dredging.
3. Take each slice of bread and butter both sides. Cut into 4 strips or leave whole.
4. Dip the strips (or the slice if leaving whole) in the egg mixture so it gets on both sides. Shake off excess and place in the bottom of the air fryer basket.
5. Remove the pan and basket from the air fryer and place on a heat resistant surface.
6. Spray the bottom of the basket with butter flavored nonstick spray. Place the dredged strips in one layer on the bottom or one full slice in the bottom. You must do this in batches. Cook for 4 minutes and open the air fryer. (My air fryer tends to cook quickly so the one side was done and crispy in 4 minutes. Other air fryers may take more time). Spray the top with the butter flavor spray and put in for 2 minutes.
7. Pull out the basket and set on a heat resistant surface. Turn the sticks or slice and spray again with butter flavored spray. Put back in the air fryer for 2 to 3 more minutes or until the side gets crispy. Watch it does not burn and sometimes it is hard to tell because the cinnamon makes the bread brown to begin with.
8. Serve with jam or syrup.

Not Your Usual Egg Rolls

These are not your usual egg rolls because they for breakfast and they are delicious and portable too. Take a few as you leave for school or work and eat them on the way. They are filled with crunchy hash browns, fluffy egg and flavorful bacon for a hearty and quick breakfast. The recipe makes 12 egg rolls and that should feed the whole family or your department at work. Serve with dipping sauce if you like. I use ketchup or maple syrup. Spice up your ketchup with a little hot sauce to get the morning rolling.

Ingredients:
6 eggs, scrambled

3 cups frozen hash browns, already browned in a skillet

8 pieces of bacon, cooked and crumbled

12 egg roll wrappers

1 cup shredded cheddar or Mozzarella

Directions:

1. Pre-scramble the eggs, brown the hash browns and cook the bacon. Let everything cool. Crumble the bacon. Do this in the morning or before you go to bed and store in the refrigerator.
2. Place each egg roll wrapper on a flat surface and divide the fillings evenly between all twelve.
3. Start with the egg, then spoon on some hash browns. Sprinkle with bacon and cheese.
4. Roll the eggrolls and dab with water at the ends and press to make them stick. Roll them tightly.
5. While filling and rolling the wrappers, preheat the air fryer to 380 degrees F for 2 minutes.
6. Remove the basket from the air fryer and place on a heat resistant surface. Spray with nonstick spray and place as many egg rolls as you can get in one layer in the basket seam side down.
7. Cook for 3 minutes, turn the eggrolls over and cook another 3 minutes.
8. Cook the rest of the egg rolls and serve.

Puff Pastry Breakfast Pockets

These little puffy pillows of delightful deliciousness are a real treat in the morning. I make them for breakfast, but they are good for lunch too. The recipe requires sausage crumbles. You can get these at the grocery store, but it is much cheaper and easy to make them. Just fry a sausage patty or two in the same pan you cook the bacon and when they are cool, cut them up in tiny pieces. The recipe makes 4 delicious pockets.

Ingredients:
5 eggs
½ cup bacon, cooked and crumbled
½ cup sausage crumbles, cooked
1 box of puff pastry sheets
½ cup shredded cheese

Directions:
1. Scramble the eggs and add the bacon and sausage. Mix well, remove from the heat and set aside to cool. This is where you cover and put in the refrigerator overnight if you would like.
2. Spread out the puff pastry on a flat, clean surface and cut into 4 equal rectangles.
3. Spoon the cooled egg mixture onto half of the rectangles.
4. Sprinkle with cheese and fold the other half of the puff pastry over top.
5. Press the edges with the tines of a fork dipped in water to make it stick.
6. Place 2 pockets in the air fryer basket that has been sprayed with nonstick spray.
7. Bake at 370 degrees F 8 to 10 minutes checking every 3 minutes to make sure they don't burn. The pockets should be golden brown and flaky when done.
8. Continue with the other two pockets and serve.

Scrambled Eggs In An Air Fryer

A metal or foil pan that fits into the air fryer is needed for this recipe. You can imagine the mess you would have if you just poured whisked eggs in the basket alone. I have used a larger ceramic ramekin too. Just be sure to spray it with nonstick spray before putting the egg mixture in. The eggs do take the shape of the container and come out kind of like a solid mass, but they are fluffy and light. This recipe makes 1 serving.

Ingredients:
1 tablespoon butter
2 eggs
salt and pepper to taste
2 tablespoons grated Parmesan cheese (optional)

Directions:
1. Preheat the air fryer to 220 degrees F for 2 minutes.
2. Place the nonstick sprayed pan or ramekin in the air fryer and add the butter. Cook for 1 minute so the butter melts.
3. In a bowl, whisk together the eggs, salt and pepper and cheese if you are using it.
4. Pour the mixture in the pan with the butter and cook 2 minutes.
5. Open and stir with a rubber spatula and close to cook one more minute.
6. I do not like runny scrambled eggs so I might put mine in for another minute. Check and see if they are done and serve immediately.

Some of these recipes can easily be adapted for lunch and even dinner but if you want some real lunch recipes, go to the next chapter.

Chapter 3: Lunches You Will Love

In this chapter different lunch specialties will abound and some just might be good enough for dinner too. There are salads, quesadillas, a variety of sandwiches, pizza, hot dogs and hamburgers all to be done in an air fryer.

Air Fried Pasta Salad

You would not think that a salad could be air fried, but some of the components in a salad are delicious when they are popped in one and roasted. This is the instance with this pasta salad. The eggplant and zucchini are air fried to give them a roasted or "grilled" flavor that is pretty spectacular in this pasta salad. This salad is great to take to pot lucks because it makes a big 16 servings. Make half of it for the family and take some for lunch to school or work. I found that ½ cup Italian dressing wasn't quite enough and 1 whole cup was too much. It depends on your taste. If there isn't enough, add a little more and mix it in before serving.

Ingredients:
3 small eggplant, sliced in 1/2-inch pieces, do not peel
2 tablespoons olive oil, divided
3 medium zucchini, sliced in ½-inch pieces, do not peel
4 medium tomatoes, sliced in eighths
1 cup cherry tomatoes, cut in half
2 bell peppers, seeded and cut in chunks
4 cups cooked, rinsed and drained pasta (I like corkscrews)

2 teaspoons salt
6 large leaves of basil, chopped
½ cup bottled Italian dressing
8 tablespoons grated Parmesan cheese

Directions:

1. Toss eggplant slices in 1 tablespoon of oil and put in the basket of the air fryer. Set for 350 degrees F and cook for 30 to 40 minutes or until soft and cooked through. Check after 20 minutes.
2. Toss the zucchini slices with the other tablespoon of oil and put in the basket of the air fryer. Cook for 15 to 20 minutes or until soft and cooked through.
3. Cut the large tomatoes and arrange in the basket of the air fryer. Spray with cooking spray and cook about 30 minutes. They should shrink and get a little brown on the edges. Cut the cherry tomatoes and bell peppers and place them in a large serving bowl. Add the cooked and drained pasta.
4. Add the roasted vegetables to the boil along with the salt, basil and Italian Dressing. Sprinkle with the Parmesan and mix in.
5. Cover and refrigerate at least 2 hours or overnight before serving.

Air Fried Quesadilla

This recipe calls for whole grain flour tortillas and you can make them with regular flour ones too. The only thing is that they must fit in the air fryer. I found 6-inch tortillas fit right in the basket. This is a vegetable/black bean quesadilla that does not have any meat at all. It also uses Greek yogurt instead of sour cream, so it is a different type of flavor. This recipe makes 4 servings.

Ingredients:
4 6-inch whole grain flour tortillas
1 cup shredded Cheddar cheese
1 cup red bell pepper, seeded and sliced
1 cup zucchini, sliced
1 cup black beans, rinsed and drained well
2 ounces plain Greek yogurt
1 teaspoon lime zest
juice of 1 lime
¼ teaspoons cumin
2 tablespoons fresh cilantro, chopped
½ cup Pico de Gallo, drained

Directions:
1. Place the tortillas on a flat surface and sprinkle half of the cheese over half of each tortilla.
2. Add some of the bell pepper and zucchini over the cheese.
3. Spoon black beans on top of the vegetables and sprinkle the rest of the cheese over the beans.
4. Fold the empty half of each tortilla over the vegetables and cheese to the other side and secure with toothpicks. Don't let the toothpicks bee too long because they will char and smoke in the air fryer.
5. Spray the inside of the air fryer basket with nonstick spray and put 2 of the quesadillas in spraying them also with the nonstick spray. Cook at 400 degrees F about 5 minutes, turn and spray the other side. Cook another 5 minutes or until the quesadilla is brown and cheese melted. Do the same with the other two quesadillas.
6. While cooking, make a sauce. In a bowl, mix the yogurt, lime zest, lime juice, cumin.

7. When quesadillas are done, cut them into wedges and sprinkle with some fresh cilantro.
8. Serve with the cumin cream and a tablespoon or two of Pico de Gallo.

Bite Size Greek Spanakopita

Spanakopita, for those who don't know what it is, is a fluffy crust made of special Greek pastry called phyllo dough and it is filled with cheese, spinach and lemon. These are mini sized and perfect for a lunch. This recipe makes 16 little bites and that is more than enough for lunch. It is possible to use this recipe as a party appetizer.

Ingredients:
2 tablespoons water
1 10-ounce package baby spinach
¼ cup feta cheese
2 tablespoons fresh grated Parmesan cheese
¼ cup 1% low fat cottage cheese
1 large egg white
1 teaspoon lemon zest
1/8 teaspoon cayenne pepper (optional)
1 teaspoon dry oregano
¼ teaspoon salt
¼ teaspoon pepper
4 13 x 18-inch sheets frozen phyllo dough, thawed

1 tablespoon olive oil

Directions:

1. Put water and spinach in a saucepan and cook over high. Stir constantly while it wilts. This should take about 5 minutes. Drain the spinach in a colander and let it cool about 10 minutes. Press with a paper towel and get rid of as much moisture as you can.
2. In a bowl combine the feta, Parmesan, cottage cheese, egg white, lemon zest, cayenne, oregano, salt and pepper and mix with a fork until it is well mixed.
3. Place 1 sheet of phyllo dough on a flat work surface and brush, with a pastry brush, lightly with olive oil. Put another sheet on to and brush again. Do the same 2 more times so you have 4 sheets stacked and oiled.
4. Use a sharp knife to cut strips eight 2 ¼-inch wide working the long side. You will create long strips. Cut the long strips in half and you will have 16 strips in all.
5. Spoon 1 tablespoon of the spinach filling onto the short end of each strip. Fold one corner over the filling to make a triangle. Keep folding back and forth to the end of the strip and it should look like a triangular packet. Continue with the other 15 strips.
6. Spray the air fryer basket with cooking spray. Put 8 of the packets in the basket with the seam side down and spray the tops with cooking spray.
7. Cook at 375 degrees F about 5 to 7 minutes, checking after 5 to make sure they are just lightly brown. Flip the packets over and cook another 5 to 7 minutes, checking after 5 to make sure they are not burning or turning too dark.
8. Serve either hot or cold.

Calzones in an Air Fryer

We call these folded pizzas because that is what you do. You make a pizza and fold it over so all the fillings are inside. I have also heard them called moon pizzas because they are in the shape of a crescent moon. They are easy to take with you for lunch to the office or school and are easily heated in a microwave or you can eat them cold. This recipe makes 4 calzones.

Ingredients:
1 teaspoon olive oil
1 clove garlic, peeled and minced
¼ cup onion, peeled and chopped
3 cups baby spinach
1/3 cup marinara sauce
2 ounces shredded meat or diced pepperoni (chicken, pork, beef)
6 ounces prepared pizza dough (regular or wheat)
6 tablespoons shredded Mozzarella cheese

Directions:
1. In a skillet, heat the oil over medium high heat and add the onion and garlic. Sauté about 2 minutes.
2. Add the spinach and stir constantly until it is wilted, about 2 more minutes. Remove the skillet from the heat and stir in the marinara and the meat.
3. Divide the dough in 4 equal pieces and roll on a floured surface to about 6-inch circles.

4. Place ¼ of the filling near the middle but off to one side of the dough circles.
5. Top with 1/4th of the cheese and fold the circle over the filling to make half circles.
6. Use a fork to crimp the open sides and seal them and poke a few holes in the top to let steam escape.
7. Place 2 of the calzones in the air fryer that has been sprayed with nonstick spray and cook at 325 degrees F about 6 minutes, flip and cook another 6 minutes.
8. Check periodically to make sure they are not turning too brown or charring.

Chinese Dumplings with Dipping Sauce

I love little dumplings when we go to our favorite Chinese restaurant. These are even better than the ones there and they aren't all that difficult to make. They are both crispy and chewy with pork and ginger flavors that are out of this world. It is also possible to serve these as an appetizer, but I find them a great lunch entrée. They are made from won ton wrappers and if you cannot find won ton wrappers, use spring roll wrappers. This recipe makes 18 dumplings.

Ingredients:
1 teaspoon canola oil

4 cups bok choy, chopped
1 tablespoon (3 cloves) peeled and chopped garlic
1 tablespoon fresh chopped ginger
4.5 ounces ground pork
¼ teaspoon red pepper flakes, crushed
18 won ton wrappers (about 3 ½ inch square)
2 teaspoons low sodium soy sauce
1 teaspoon toasted sesame oil
2 tablespoons rice vinegar
½ teaspoon packed light brown sugar
1 tablespoon green onion, finely chopped

Directions:
1. In a skillet, heat the canola oil and add the bok choy over medium heat. Sauté until it is wilted and dry, about 6 minutes.
2. Add the garlic and the ginger and cook stirring constantly for about 1 minute. Pour into a plate to cool for at least 5 minutes and pat the mixture dry with paper towels.
3. In a bowl, mix the ground pork, bok choy mixture and the red pepper flakes.
4. Place a won ton wrapper on a flat surface and spoon about 1 tablespoon of the pork mixture into the center. Lightly moisten the edges of the wrapper with water and fold to make a half moon shape. Pinch edges to seal.
5. Spray the air fryer basket with nonstick spray. Place 6 dumplings in the basket making sure there is a little room between each. Spray the dumplings with cooking spray and cook at 375 degrees for 5 minutes, turn, coat with more spray and cook another 5 minutes. If the dumplings are not lightly browned, go another 2 minutes.
6. Repeat with remaining dumplings.
7. While the dumplings are cooking, make a sauce by stirring together the soy sauce, sesame oil, rice vinegar, brown sugar and green peppers. Stir until sugar dissolves and serve with the dumplings.

Buffalo Fried Chicken Sandwich

This chicken sandwich is spicy and delicious and made with chicken thighs, so it is also tender inside and juicy. The chicken needs to marinate about 24 hours so make sure to start it the night before. This makes 4 chicken sandwiches and you must cook the chicken in two batches.

Ingredients:
¼ to ½ bottle of buffalo sauce, enough to cover the chicken
4 boneless, skinless chicken thighs
1 cup flour
1 teaspoon garlic powder
1 teaspoon dried thyme
1 teaspoon onion powder
1 teaspoon chipotle powder
1 teaspoon paprika
1 teaspoon salt
1 teaspoon pepper
lettuce, buns, mayo and pickles for condiments on the sandwich

Directions:
1. Place the chicken in a shallow pan and cover with the buffalo sauce. Cover with plastic wrap and put in the refrigerator 24 hours.
2. In a deep dish pie pan, combine the flour, garlic powder, thyme, onion powder, chipotle powder, paprika, salt and pepper and whisk well.
3. Shake some of the buffalo sauce off the chicken and dredge it in the flour mixture. Put two thighs at a time in the air fryer basket that has been sprayed with nonstick spray.
4. Set for 390 degrees F and fry for 15 minutes shaking pan every 5 minutes so it does not stick. Test with a meat thermometer to make sure the chicken is done. It should read 165 degrees F.
5. Repeat with the other two chicken thighs.
6. Place the thighs on a bun and garnish with lettuce, may and a pickle.

Corned Beef Reuben Sandwich

Making a Rueben in an air fryer is a very easy process. You make the sandwich, put it in the air fryer and let it go flipping it so both sides are toasted. If you do not like sauerkraut, leave that off and have it without or substitute with coleslaw. I add my coleslaw after the sandwich is cooked and I still use a little of the Russian Dressing. This recipe makes 4 sandwiches and you must cook them individually, one at a time in the air fryer.

Ingredients:
8 slices of rye bread
¼ cup Russian Dressing
1 pound corned beef, sliced thin
12 ounces of canned, jarred or bagged sauerkraut, drained, squeezed and pat dry with a paper towel
4 slices of Swiss cheese

Directions:
1. Spread the Russian dressing equally on 4 pieces of the bread.
2. Place corned beef on top of the dressing.
3. Spoon drained and dried sauerkraut on top.
4. Place a piece of Swiss cheese on top of the sauerkraut.
5. Add the top piece of bread.
6. Spray the top and bottom with nonstick butter flavor spray (or you can spread with a little soft butter instead, and place one sandwich in the air fryer basket.
7. Cook at 390 degrees for 4 minutes. Flip the sandwich and cook another 3 to 4 minutes.
8. Repeat with rest of sandwiches.

Fried Chicken Sandwich

Try this with delicious Pickle Juice

This is a crispy fried chicken sandwich with a bunch of flavor. It tastes remarkably like the ones you get at Chick-Fil-A and this recipe makes 2 of them. There is a bunch of different herbs and spices in this recipe and that is what gives it such good flavor along with a surprise ingredient, pickle juice. Start with plenty of time because the chicken marinates in the pickle juice for at least 30 minutes. There is an option to make the chicken sandwich spicy; add ¼ teaspoon cayenne pepper.

Ingredients:
2 boneless, skinless chicken breasts
½ cup dill pickle juice
2 eggs
½ cup milk
1 cup flour
2 tablespoons powder sugar
½ teaspoon garlic powder
½ teaspoon ground celery seed
1 teaspoon paprika
1 teaspoon sea salt
½ teaspoon fresh ground pepper

1 tablespoon olive oil in a mist bottle or olive oil nonstick spray
4 toasted hamburger buns, buttered
8 dill pickle chips

Directions:
1. Place the chicken breasts between 2 pieces of wax paper and pound to about ½ inch thick.
2. Place chicken into a zip-lock bag with the pickle juice and marinate in the refrigerator at least 30 minutes.
3. Beat the egg in a bowl with the milk.
4. In a big bowl whisk the flour, powder sugar and all the herbs and spices.
5. Dip the chicken breast in the egg, then in the flour mixture. Makes sure they are completely coated. Shake off the excess flour.
6. Spray the bottom of the basket and put one breast in spraying the chicken with the olive oil or nonstick olive oil flavored spray.
7. Cook 340 degrees for 6 minutes and use tongs to flip and spray with more oil. Cook 6 more minutes. Raise the temperature to 400 degrees and cook 2 more minutes.
8. Repeat with the other chicken breast.
9. Serve on buttered toasted buns with 2 pickle chips and maybe some mayo if you want.

Fried Fish Sandwich

It is super easy to make this fish sandwich. All you need is some code, flour, breadcrumbs and olive oil spray to make a delicious sandwich. Use tartar sauce on fresh toasted Kaiser rolls and you have a lunch fit for a sea captain. This recipe makes 4 sandwiches.

Ingredients:
2 tablespoons flour
¼ teaspoon salt
1/8 teaspoon pepper
¼ teaspoon Old Bay Seasoning (optional)
¾ cup unseasoned breadcrumbs
4 small cod fillets, without skin
olive oil in a spray bottle or olive oil flavored nonstick spray
A few lemon wedges

Directions:
1. Combine the flour, salt, pepper and Old Bay seasoning in a bowl.
2. Place the bread crumbs in another bowl.
3. Dredge the fillets in the flour mixture and then in the breadcrumbs.
4. Preheat the air fryer to 390 degrees F for 3 minutes.
5. Spray the inside basket with nonstick spray.
6. Place two of the dredged fillets in the basket of the air fryer and cook for 15 minutes, flipping halfway through.
7. Repeat with the other two fillets.
8. Serve on a toasted bun with a squeeze of lemon juice and some tartar sauce.

Green Salad with Luscious Roasted Red Peppers

This salad is delicious but this recipe is more to teach you how to roast red peppers. The salad is easy to make and you can add just about anything to it. The only thing you are cooking in the air fryer is the red peppers. This makes 4 servings of salad.

Ingredients:
1 red bell pepper
3 tablespoons plain yogurt

1 tablespoon lemon juice

2 tablespoons olive oil

1/8 teaspoon salt

1 pinch ground pepper

1 head Romaine lettuce

2 cups fresh baby spinach leaves

Directions:

1. Preheat the air fryer to 390 degrees F for 3 minutes.
2. Do not do anything to the red pepper except wash it off and dry it.
3. Place it in the basket of the air fryer and set timer for 8 minutes. Check and see if the skin is slightly charred. If not, put it in for 2 minutes at a time until it is charred.
4. Place the pepper in a small bowl and cover the bowl with plastic wrap. Set it aside for 10 to 15 minutes.
5. There should be liquid in the bowl. Reserve 2 tablespoons of it.
6. Cut the pepper in half and remove the seeds. Remove the skin that should be easy to peel off.
7. Cut the pepper into strips.
8. Place the liquid from the pepper in a bowl with the yogurt, lemon juice and olive oil and whisk. Add the salt and pepper and combine.
9. Place the lettuce and spinach in a salad bowl and toss. Add the yogurt mixture and the pepper strips and toss to coat.
10. Serve immediately.

Grill Flavored Hamburgers

The neat thing about an air fryer is that it simulates a grill. When you add liquid smoke to a recipe it tastes even more like it was grilled. Even in the dead of winter you can have what tastes and looks like a grilled hamburger. Here is a little trick to make perfect hamburgers in the air fryer. Push the center of each burger patty down so it makes an indentation with your thumb in the middle. This stops all the juices from gathering in the middle and helps them distribute throughout the burger. This makes 4 patties but it is very simple to double the recipe.

Ingredients:
½ teaspoon garlic powder
½ teaspoon onion powder
1 teaspoon dried parsley
½ teaspoon salt
½ teaspoon black pepper
1 tablespoon Worcestershire sauce
2 drops liquid smoke
1 pound ground beef

Directions:
1. In a bowl combine the garlic powder, onion powder, parsley, salt and pepper and whisk with a wire whisk.
2. Add the Worcestershire sauce and liquid smoke and mix in well.

3. Drop in the ground beef and mix with your hands until everything is well combined.
4. Form 4 hamburger patties and place two of them in the basket of the air fryer that has been sprayed with nonstick butter flavored spray.
5. Spray the top of the patties with the spray and cook at 350 degrees for 10 minutes. There is no need to flip them.
6. Check with a meat thermometer to make sure they say 160 degrees F. If jot, put the patties in for another few minutes.
7. Serve on buns with condiments.

Healthier Hot Dogs

Hot dogs are easy to make in an air fryer and I think they taste better. They aren't waterlogged like they are when you boil them and they don't get charred like they do when you grill them. The grease collects in the bottom of the air fryer and you don't consume it. In just a few minutes they are ready to go. This recipe is for 2 hot dogs but you can make more. Three fit in the basket of the air fryer nicely with some room between them.

Ingredients:
2 hot dogs
2 buns
2 tablespoons grated Cheddar cheese

Directions:
1. Preheat the air fryer to 390 degrees for 4 minutes.

2. Place 2 hot dogs in the basket at a time maybe 3.
3. Cook for 5 minutes.
4. Use tongs to remove the hot dogs from the basket, put in a bun, sprinkle with 1 tablespoon of the shredded cheese and put on some condiments.
5. Repeat with more hot dogs.

Hot and Delicious Chicken Salad

I make this when I have left over cooked chicken and take it to lunch at work. It is very delicious and different, since no one thinks of chicken salad as being hot. This makes 1 serving.

Ingredients:
½ cup celery, chopped
2 tablespoons green onion, chopped
¼ teaspoon garlic powder
¼ teaspoon onion powder
2 to 3 tablespoons softened cream cheese, more if you like
1/8 teaspoon cracked black pepper
1 cooked chicken breast, shredded
½ cup shredded cheddar, divided

Directions:
1. Preheat the air fryer to 350 degrees F for about 2 minutes.
2. In a bowl, mix the celery, green onion, garlic powder, onion powder, cream cheese and black pepper. Mix well with a fork.
3. Add the chicken and half of the shredded cheddar and mix again.
4. Spray a pan or ramekin that fits inside the basket of the air fryer with nonstick spray. I use a 4 or 5 inch cake pan.
5. Bake in the air fryer about 3 to 4 minutes and open the air fryer.
6. Sprinkle the remaining cheese over top and return to baking about 1 to 2 minutes or until the cheese melts and browns a little.
7. Serve immediately.

Hot Ham and Cheese Sandwich

Use a Croissant Instead Of Kaiser Roll If Desired

These are great sandwiches for any time, but I tend to make them for New Year's Eve because they are so easy to make. You can put 2 at a time in the air fryer and they come out perfectly hot and melty with a delicious onion like flavor. You can also try making them with mayonnaise and horseradish and use roast beef and provolone cheese. This recipe makes 4 sandwiches.

Ingredients:
4 Kaiser buns, split
12 ounces thin sliced deli ham
4 slices Swiss cheese
4 slices of cooked and crumbled bacon
2 tablespoons mayonnaise
2 teaspoons Dijon Mustard
½ teaspoon Worcestershire sauce
Sliced tomato (optional)

Directions:
1. Preheat the air fryer to 350 degrees for about 2 minutes.
2. Tear off 4 squares of aluminum foil that will wrap the sandwiches and set on a flat surface.

3. Place the bottom of the buns on each square of foil in the middle.
4. Divide the ham evenly between the buns and place on top the bottom bun part.
5. Top with a slice of Swiss on each bun.
6. Sprinkle the crumbled bacon over the cheese on each bun.
7. In a small bowl, combine the mayonnaise, Dijon Mustard and Worcestershire sauce and mix well.
8. Spread on the top inside of each bun. You should use it all.
9. Place that top bun on the sandwich and completely wrap in the aluminum foil.
10. Place 2 in the air fryer and cook for 10 minutes.
11. Remove from air fryer with tongs and set aside to cool a few minutes.
12. Place the other 2 sandwiches in and cook another 10 minutes and let cool.
13. Open the foil. The cheese should be melty and the sandwich hot. Remove the top bun and put a tomato on top if desired.
14. Serve while hot.

Light and Airy Empanadas

These empanadas are a flavor explosion with ground beef, mushrooms and olives. You do need square Gyoza wrappers and can usually find them in the Spanish or Mexican section of the grocery store. This makes 4 empanadas and serves 2 people.

Ingredients:

1 tablespoon olive oil
3 ounces ground beef, lean
¼ cup white onion, peeled and chopped fine
3 ounces cremini mushrooms, chopped fine
5 pitted green olives, chopped
¼ teaspoon paprika
2 teaspoons garlic, peeled and finely chopped
1/8 teaspoon ground cinnamon
¼ teaspoon ground cumin
½ cup chopped tomatoes
8 square gyoza wrappers
1 large egg, lightly beaten

Directions:

1. Heat the olive oil in a skillet over medium heat and brown the beef with the onion about 3 to 4 minutes.
2. Add the mushrooms and cook until they start to turn brown, about 5 to 6 minutes.
3. Add the olives, paprika, garlic, cinnamon and cumin and cook 3 more minutes.
4. Add the tomato and cook 2 minutes. Let the mixture in the skillet cool 5 minutes.
5. Place gyoza wrappers on a flat surface and fill, in the center with 1 ½ tablespoons of the skillet mixture.
6. Dab some of the beaten egg around the edges of the square, fold over and seal.
7. Spray the air fryer with butter flavor nonstick spray and place 2 of the empanadas in.
8. Cook at 400 degrees F for 7 minutes or until they are brown.
9. Repeat with other 2 empanadas.

Mexican Taquitos

Use cooked and shredded pork or chicken to make these bundles of goodness. They are small, easy to pack in a lunch and pack a punch of flavor. This recipe makes 10 taquitos. Dip in salsa and/or sour cream for a real treat.

Ingredients:
30 ounces of cooked shred pork or chicken
1 lime
10 small flour tortillas
2 ½ cups shredded mozzarella cheese

Directions:
1. Preheat the air fryer to 380 degrees for about 4 minutes.
2. Put the cooked shredded meat in a bowl and squeeze the juice of the whole lime over top. Toss to coat.\
3. Take 5 of the 10 tortillas and wrap them in a damp paper towel. Place in the microwave and microwave on high 10 seconds and check. This is to make the tortillas soft and flexible so they can easily be rolled.
4. Place 3 ounces of the meat and divide half the cheese between the 5 tortillas. Roll them up and tuck in the sides.
5. Spray the inside basket of the air fryer with nonstick spray and place the 5 taquitos inside. Spray the tops of the taquitos with spray and cook 5 minutes, flip and cook another 5 minutes or until they are lightly browned.
6. Do the same with the other 5 tortillas.

7. Serve with salsa and sour cream.

Monti Cristo Sandwich with Raspberry Sauce

I had my first Monti Cristo sandwich at a fancy restaurant at 12 years old when my aunt and uncle took my mom out for her birthday. It was one of the cheapest things on the menu, so I did not think it was going to be all that great. I was wrong. Monti Cristo sandwiches are sweet and savory. They are filled with ham, turkey and Swiss cheese (which I love) and the whole sandwich is dredged in a batter and deep fried. They are not healthy but delicious. The air fryer makes them a little healthier because they do not soak up all that oil and this sandwich tastes remarkably delicious. The outside is a little crispy but the inside is moist because of the cheese. Be prepared to be transported to food heaven. The recipe makes 1 sandwich.

Ingredients:
1 egg
½ teaspoon vanilla extract
3 tablespoons half and half
2 slices sourdough or multigrain bread (thicker slices than white bread)
2 ounces deli ham, thin sliced
2 ounces deli turkey, thin sliced
2 ½ ounces Swiss cheese slices
1 teaspoon butter, melted
Powder sugar, optional
Raspberry jam

Directions:
1. Preheat the air fryer to 350 for 4 minutes.
2. In a deep dish pie pan, whisk the egg, vanilla and the half and half until well combined and set aside.
3. Place one slice of bread on a clean cutting board. Top with the ham and the turkey.
4. Place a slice of Swiss on top and cover with the other piece of bread. Press down to compress just a little.

5. Rip off a piece of aluminum foil a little bigger than the sandwich and brush with the melted butter. There should be some butter left over.
6. Place the whole sandwich in the egg mixture and let it soak it up for about 30 seconds. Flip and let the other side soak 30 seconds.
7. Place the sandwich on the buttered foil and transfer foil and all to the basket of the air fryer.
8. Brush the top of the sandwich with a little more of the melted butter.
9. Cook for 10 minutes and open the air fryer and carefully, with a spatula, flip the sandwich over. You must be careful so you do not tear the foil (I use heavy duty foil).
10. Brush this side of the sandwich with more of the butter and fry 8 minutes.
11. Remove the sandwich from the air fryer and place on a plate before sprinkling with powder sugar.
12. Put the raspberry jam in a small bowl and serve it on the side to dip the sandwich in as you eat it.

Perfect Grilled Cheese with Options

Grilled cheese sandwiches are an American classic. Have them plain or add things to them to make them tasty and unique. In an air fryer, the bread gets very crispy and the cheese is delightfully melty. One thing I did find out is the top slice of bread tends to fly off during the air frying and sits on the side, vertically against the side of the basket because the force of the air. I stick 2 toothpicks on either end of the sandwich and use kitchen shears to cut them short. I left them long one time and everything smoked up because the toothpick caught a flame. I was lucky I stayed with the air fryer while I was making them or it all would gone poof. This recipe makes 1 serving. Make cheddar sandwiches with crumbled bacon and/or sliced mushrooms or try Provolone slices with soft Mozzarella and a thin slice of tomato with basil leaves on top. I love gouda with bacon or a slice of thin deli ham or Swiss with basil leaves on rye.

Ingredients:
2 slices bread (your favorite)
2 to 3 slices Cheddar cheese (or Swiss, Mozzarella, Gouda or other harder cheese)
2 teaspoons softened butter
Options:
cooked crumbled bacon
Sliced tomato
basil leaves
mushrooms
deli ham or turkey

Directions:
1. Spread the butter on one side of the bread. This is the outside of the sandwich and the inside is unbuttered. I put the bread on a piece of wax paper.
2. Place the cheese on the bread and any of the options.
3. Butter the other slice of bread and place the unbuttered side face down on top of the filling.
4. Preheat the air fryer to 370 degrees for 2 minutes.

5. Place the toothpicks in the sandwich and trim so they only come up a little higher than the sandwich.
6. Use a plastic spatula to transfer the sandwich to the nonstick sprayed basket of the air fryer.
7. Cook 4 minutes, flip and cook another 4 minutes and serve.

Quick and Delicious Pita Pizza

You will need a stainless steel trivet that fits inside the air fryer that has short legs. The idea is to weigh the pizza down so that the toppings don't fly off with the force of the air in the air fryer. It can get messy if you don't do this. Be careful not to scratch the nonstick surface of the inside basket. Put whatever you want on your pizza. I like sausage and I precook it before putting it on. This makes 1 pizza.

Ingredients:
1 pita
1 tablespoon pizza sauce or alfredo sauce
Toppings: cooked sausage, pepperoni, onion, mushrooms, peppers, etc.
¼ cup shredded Mozzarella cheese
1 drizzle of olive oil

Directions:
1. Preheat the air fryer to 350 degrees for 2 to 3 minutes.
2. Place the pita on a flat surface and use a spoon to apply the pizza sauce and swirl it from the middle to the edges.

3. Add toppings and cheese and drizzle a little olive oil over the top of the pizza.
4. Spray the inside basket of the air fryer with nonstick spray and place the pita pizza in.
5. Rip off a piece of foil about the same size as the pizza and spray one side with nonstick spray. Place the sprayed side face down on top of the pizza.
6. Place the trivet upside down so the legs are in the air on top of the foil.
7. Cook for about 6 minutes, checking after 4 to make sure it isn't burning. The trivet will be hot, use tongs to remove it and put it on a heat resistant surface. Carefully remove the pizza from the basket and take off the foil.
8. Cut in 2 to 4 pieces and serve.

Some of these lunch recipes are easily adapted to party food and appetizers. The same goes for the next chapter on appetizers. They can interchangeably be used for lunches.

Chapter 4 : Savory Appetizers and Sweet Snacks

You can make your own snacks in your air fryer in just a few minutes and they will be fresh and tasty. This chapter includes recipes for chips including banana and apple. There are recipes for wings and macaroni and cheese balls. Try some Parmesan dill pickles or fried ravioli and wontons. You will be the master of the kitchen when you create these appetizers and snacks made in an air fryer.

Banana Chips

Banana chips are super easy to create and are a great snack for toddlers all the way to adults. These have turmeric powder, which is good for you and it turns the chips a pretty yellow. Soaking them in the water with turmeric and salt will keep the slices from turning black.

Ingredients:
3 bananas, peeled and cut into slices
enough water to cover the banana slices
1 teaspoon salt
½ teaspoon turmeric
1 tablespoon coconut oil

Directions:

1. Slice the peeled bananas and put them into a bowl with enough water to cover them, salt and turmeric that has been blended together. I put a saucer or plate over top to keep the slices submerged. Let them soak about 5 to 10 minutes.
2. Drain the banana slices in a colander. Prepare a baking sheet with a couple paper towels lining it. Pour the banana slices on and spread around. Take more paper towels and press down getting as much of the water off them as possible without damaging them.
3. Preheat the air fryer to 350 degrees F for about 2 minutes. Open and spray with nonstick spray.
4. Place the dried banana chips in a bowl and toss with the coconut oil. Place them in the air fryer basket in a single layer (you will have to do batches) and bake for 10 to 15 minutes. They should be crispy when they are done.
5. Sprinkle with a little salt if desired and serve warm or cold. Keep extras in an air tight container and they will last about 5 to 7 days.

Blossoming Onion

This recipe makes one of those famous fried onions from the popular Aussie restaurant most of us know. It is not laden with oil, however and is very delicious. I like using the panko bread crumbs because they get very crunchy and the buttermilk gives it great flavor and helps the breadcrumbs to stick because it is so thick. Vidalia onions are very sweet, but you can only get them at certain times of year. Substitute a Texas sweet onion the rest of the year. This makes one blossoming onion.

Ingredients:

1/3 cup all-purpose flour
1 tablespoon buttermilk
2 large eggs, beaten
1/3 cup panko breadcrumbs
1 ½ teaspoon Old Bay seafood seasoning
1 large Vidalia onion, peeled
olive oil in a spray container

Directions:

1. Place the flour in a bowl that is big enough to accommodate the whole onion and set aside.
2. Whisk the buttermilk and eggs in another bowl and set it aside.
3. Mix the breadcrumbs and seafood seasoning in a third bowl and set aside.
4. To prepare the onion, trim the top so you make a flat surface on which the onion can sit but leave the root end alone. Turn the onion so it sits on this flat end and the root end is toward you.
5. Cut the onion in 4 wedges without piercing the root and cut each wedge in half also not piercing the root. Repeat until wedges are about ¼ inch thick.
6. Turn the onion over and separate the layers. The onion should resemble a blooming flower with layers of petals if you do it right. The root end keeps it intact.
7. Hold the onion by the root end and dip it in the flour making sure it gets in all the nooks and crannies. I turn it over and sprinkle more on it. Shake off excess.
8. Hold by the root end again and dip it into the egg mixture moving and swirling it around so the egg and buttermilk get deep into the petals.
9. Place the onion in the panko bread crumbs with the petals up and use fingers to sprinkle the crumbs in between and up the onion petals.

10. Spray the basket of the air fryer with nonstick spray and place the onion in so it sits on the flat end. Spray the petals with the sprayable olive oil.
11. Cook at 400 degrees F for 10 minutes. Check after 7 minutes to make sure it isn't getting too brown. '
12. Serve with dip.

Bow Tie Pasta Chips

You can make delicious chips with pasta bow ties. Kids love these, but I do too because they are very flavorful and remind me of a cheese cracker. This recipe makes about 2 cups of chips and you will want them over and over again. You can store them in an airtight container for about a week, but they won't last that long. This is made with nutritional yeast to make it more nutritious but you do not have to use it. It does not affect the flavor at all. Get nutritional yeast at your local whole foods store.

Ingredients:
2 cups dry whole wheat bow tie pasta
1 tablespoon olive oil
1 ½ teaspoon Italian Seasoning
1 tablespoon nutritional yeast
½ teaspoon salt

Directions:
1. Cook the pasta in boiling water for half the time it states on the package instructions. Drain the pasta well and put it in a bowl.
2. Toss the pasta with the olive oil, Italian Seasoning, nutritional yeast and salt.
3. Place half the mixture in the air fryer basket that has been treated with nonstick spray.
4. Air fry at 390 degrees for 5 minutes. Pull out the basket and shake it well, put it back in and cook another 3 to 5 minutes or until the bow ties are crunchy. They will get crisper as they cool.
5. Continue with the rest of the bow ties.

Breadcrumb Stuffed Mushrooms

Stuffed mushrooms are a favorite of mine and these are very good, easy to make and come out perfect in the air fryer. The recipe makes 12 stuffed mushrooms and you do have to make them in batches. Keep them warm until they are all cooked by placing in a pan covered with foil in a preheated 350 degree oven.

Ingredients:
12 mushrooms, caps removed stems chopped
½ cup breadcrumbs
½ teaspoon salt
½ teaspoon pepper
4 tablespoons olive oil

Directions:
1. Place the caps of the mushrooms aside and chop the stems putting the chopped stems in a bowl.
2. Add the breadcrumbs, salt and pepper to the bowl and mix.
3. Add the olive oil to the bowl and mix well.
4. Preheat the air fryer to 360 degrees F and let it go 2 minutes.
5. Divide the filling evenly between the mushroom caps and fill them in.
6. Spray the basket of the air fryer with nonstick spray and with tongs, place as many mushrooms in without overlapping.

7. Cook for 10 minutes and remove from the air fryer. Before putting the next batch in, spray with nonstick spray and cook as before.

Buttermilk Chicken Bites

Use the buttermilk you bought to make the blossoming onion in this recipe. It makes the crunchiest and most delicious chicken bites I have ever had. You will never get them in a fast food restaurant again when you see how easy they are to make. These can be frozen and reheated in the air fryer at the same temperature for a little more time turning them once.

Ingredients:
1 pound chicken breast
1 tablespoon hot sauce (less if you wish or opt for none)
1 cup buttermilk
1 cup all-purpose flour
2 eggs, beaten
1 cup panko bread crumbs
1 teaspoon garlic powder
1 teaspoon cayenne (this can also be omitted)
½ teaspoon salt
½ teaspoon pepper

Directions:

1. Cut the chicken in 1-inch pieces and place in a resealable bag with the hot sauce and buttermilk. Let marinate in the refrigerator 30 minutes to 2 hours.
2. Place the flour in one bowl.
3. Beat the eggs in another bowl.
4. Mix the panko, garlic powder, cayenne, salt and pepper in another bowl.
5. Remove the chicken from the refrigerator and dip each marinated piece in the flour coating it completely.
6. Dip it in the egg and then in the panko mixture covering it completely.
7. Place on a baking sheet until they are all done.
8. Spray the basket of the air fryer with butter or olive oil flavored spray.
9. Place the bites in, as many will fit without overlapping.
10. Set for 370 degrees F and cook for 10 minutes. Flip the bites over and cook another 5 minutes. Remove from air fryer and finish the rest of the bites.
11. Serve with dipping sauce; ranch, BBQ or honey are the best.

Chinese Shrimp Toast

I used to love shrimp toast we got at the Chinese restaurant before our meals. No one serves them anymore, much to my dismay. But I found a way to make my own and it is better than those Styrofoam look a-likes any day. You use real bread and the thing that makes them great is the potato starch used in the ingredients. You do need an oil mister and some canola oil to make them taste right, canola oil flavored nonstick spray doesn't do the trick. You do have to make one slice of bread at a time. This recipe makes 24 pieces of the most delightful shrimp toast ever.

Ingredients:
4 to 6 slices white bread (use sandwich bread)
Canola oil in a mister
8 ounces of shrimp, peeled and deveined
1 egg
1 tablespoon fresh parsley

1 tablespoon mayonnaise
2 teaspoons potato starch
1 teaspoon fresh grated ginger
½ teaspoon soy sauce
¼ teaspoon sesame oil
¼ teaspoon fish sauce
toasted sesame seeds

Directions:

1. Spray one side of the bread with canola oil and place it in the air fryer basket with the oil side up.
2. Set for 370 degrees and cook 2 minutes. You will need to generously spray the bread to weight it down so it doesn't flip up in the air fryer. It still might.
3. Place the shrimp, egg, parsley, mayonnaise, potato starch, ginger, soy sauce, sesame oil and fish sauce in a food processor and process to a paste.
4. Remove the toast with tongs and place on a clean work surface so the oiled side is facing down.
5. Spread the shrimp paste evenly all the way to the edge.
6. Pour sesame seeds on a flat plat and press the slice with the shrimp side down into the seeds.
7. Cut each piece of bread in 4 triangles or sticks and put into the air fryer basket that has been sprayed with nonstick spray. Place them shrimp side up and spray with the canola oil spray.
8. Cook at 330 degrees F for 4 to 5 minutes or until the shrimp turns pink and bread is crusty.

Note: I make all the toast first and then spread with the shrimp mixture. Then I put 4 pieces in the basket at ones to fry.

Cinnamon Apple Chips

You can find apple chips at the grocery store, but they often have way too much sugar or cinnamon on them. When you make your own you can regulate how much sugar is used. These are delicious and very simple to make in the air fryer. I use a pie apple to make them like McIntosh, but Gala work well too. Store them in an air tight container for about 5 days.

Ingredients:
6 large apples
1 tablespoon lemon juice
1 teaspoon olive or coconut oil
½ cup granulated sugar
1 shake of cinnamon

Directions:
1. Peel and core the apple. Slice into wedges and put them in a bowl.
2. Pour in the lemon juice and olive oil and mix with your hand so the slices are all coated. The lemon juice keeps the apple from turning brown.
3. Spray the air fryer basket with nonstick spray. Place some apple slices in the basket so they do not overlap much.
4. Cook at 380 degrees for about 10 minutes. Remove the basket and shake about half way through.
5. Remove the basket and pour out the apple chips onto a plate. They should be crisp but will crisp even more as they cool.

6. Combine the sugar and cinnamon in a bowl and dump the chips in while still warm. Coat them with some of the sugar mixture and shake off excess. They are ready to eat.
7. Continue with the next batch making sure you do not forget to spray the basket with nonstick spray each time.

*Note: you can do this with just about any hard fruit or vegetable. Try pears with cinnamon and sugar or zucchini with a little salt and sage. Beets are good with a little salt as is summer squash.

Cheesy Spinach Roll Ups

These little rolls are made with puff pastry and make about 2 dozen or so. I'm always amazed at people who are afraid of working with puff pastry. It comes frozen in the freezer section of your supermarket. You just take it out, roll it out or roll things in it and use a knife to cut them. It isn't hard, so don't let puff pastry prevent you from making these. You will be missing out.

Ingredients:
1 sheet puff pastry
2 packages fresh baby spinach, washed and chopped
1 small clove garlic, peeled and chopped
1 ½ cups ricotta cheese
2/3 cup grated Parmesan cheese
1 cup shredded mozzarella cheese
¼ teaspoon nutmeg
salt and pepper to taste
egg wash
2 tablespoons sesame seeds

Directions:
1. Remove the puff pastry from the freezer and let it sit on the counter, in the box, while you prepare the filling.
2. Wash and dry the spinach by pressing with paper towels. Once dry, roughly chop it and put it in a large bowl with the garlic.
3. Add the ricotta, Parmesan and mozzarella and mix in.
4. Add the nutmeg, salt and pepper and combine well.

5. Roll the puff pastry onto a clean flat surface and cut with a sharp knife into 3 rectangles.
6. Spread the spinach filling on each of the rectangles, dividing it evenly.
7. Use a pastry brush to apply the egg wash to the edges of the rectangles and roll the filling into the puff pastry. You will have something that looks like 3 puffy egg rolls.
8. Place the rolls on a plate seam down and cover with plastic wrap. Refrigerate 20 minutes before continuing.
9. Preheat the air fryer to 330 degrees for about 4 minutes.
10. Remove the rolls from the refrigerator and cut each roll in 3 or 4-inch slices. Brush with the egg wash and sprinkle sesame seeds over.
11. Place as many roll slices as you can without overlapping into a nonstick sprayed air fryer basket. Bake for 4 to 5 minutes, flip them over and bake another 2 to 5 minutes. Watch because they burn easily.
12. Keep the finished rolls warm in an oven while you air fry the others. Serve hot.

Crispy Chicken Wings

You want a super easy recipe for wings, here it is. There isn't much to this recipe except to shake on a little salt and pepper and air fry the wings. Serve with ranch or barbeque sauce and you are done. Do not dump all the wings in at once. This will take two batches and the wings should not be laying over top each other.

You need to do them in a single layer. These are so crispy, it is hard to believe they are so easy.

Ingredients:
2 pounds chicken wings
salt and pepper to taste
BBQ or Ranch dressing for dip

Directions:
1. Preheat the air fryer to 380 degrees f for about 3 minutes.
2. Salt and pepper the wings.
3. Place them in a single layer on the bottom of a nonstick sprayed air fryer basket.
4. Set for 24 minutes. At 13 minutes, open the air fryer and use tongs to turn each wing.
5. When time is up, increase the temperature to 400 degrees F and bake 5 more minutes or until the skin is brown and crispy.
6. Repeat with rest of wings.

Fried Mac and Cheese Balls

These are crispy on the outside and delightfully cheesy and moist on the inside. Double the recipe because you will need more of them. This recipe makes 25 balls and your guests will beg for more.

Ingredients:

2 cups Elbow Macaroni cooked

3 pieces bacon

3 cloves garlic, peeled and chopped

3 tablespoons flour

¾ cup milk

½ can of beer

¼ cup grated Parmesan cheese

1 ½ cups shredded cheddar cheese

Salt and pepper to taste (I add a little cayenne)

3 eggs

½ cup flour

½ cup bread crumbs

Directions:

1. Cook the macaroni per package directions, drain and let cool.
2. In a frying pan, fry up the bacon until it crisps. Remove the bacon and drain on paper towels.
3. Add the garlic to the grease in the frying pan and cook for about 2 minutes.
4. Add the 3 tablespoons flour and whisk to make a thick paste.
5. Crumble the bacon and add to the paste. Stir in well.
6. Pour in the beer and milk into the frying pan and whisk constantly about 5 minutes or until a sauce starts to thicken.
7. Add salt and pepper and then add the Parmesan and cheddar stirring until everything melts.
8. Pour the cooked macaroni into a deep dish pie dish and pour the cheese sauce over. Stir until completely coated, cover with plastic wrap and put in the refrigerator for 45 minutes.
9. Remove the macaroni from the refrigerator and take a teaspoon or tablespoon full and roll it into a ball. Place balls on a baking sheet until they are all done.
10. Place the eggs in a bowl and whisk them up well.
11. Place the flour in another bowl.
12. Place the bread crumbs in yet another bowl.
13. Take one ball and roll it in the flour, covering it completely. Shake off excess.
14. Dip the ball into the egg wash making sure all sides are covered and then roll in the bread crumbs. Press them in.
15. Preheat the air fryer to 390 degrees F for 3 minutes.

16. Spray the basket with nonstick spray and put as many of the balls in as you can without them being on top of one another.
17. Bake for 10 minutes, checking after 5 to make sure they are not burning. They are done when crispy and brown. Keep the cooked ones warm in a 350 degree oven until they are all cooked and serve.

Fried Ravioli

This is an easy recipe because you get frozen mini cheese ravioli to make it and just bread it and fry it. It makes about 18 to 20 mini ravioli appetizers that will go over good at your next tailgate party.

Ingredients:
1 egg, beaten
1 cup Panko breadcrumbs
½ bag mini cheese raviolis (about 18 to 20)
1 teaspoon Italian seasoning
¼ cup fresh grated Parmesan cheese
1 cup marinara sauce, warmed for dip

Directions:

1. Preheat the air fryer to 380 degrees F for 2 minutes.
2. Whisk the egg in one bowl.
3. Place the panko bread crumbs in another bowl.
4. Dip one frozen (do not thaw) ravioli into the egg and dredge it in breadcrumbs.
5. Place in the basket of the air fryer that has been sprayed with nonstick olive oil or butter spray.
6. Repeat until the basket is full without any raviolis overlapping.
7. Cook for 12 minutes and flipping the raviolis after 6 minutes.
8. The ravioli will be light brown and crispy when they are done.
9. Serve with warm marinara sauce as a dip.

Homemade Jalapeno Poppers

When you work with jalapeno peppers, or any hot pepper, wear gloves so the chemical in the seeds does not irritate your skin. If you do get some on your hands or anywhere else, just dab with milk to stop the burning. This makes 20 poppers and uses 10

peppers. They are filled with cream cheese and parsley and are spicy and delicious.

Ingredients:
10 jalapeno peppers
8 ounces cream cheese, at room temperature
¼ cup fresh parsley
¾ cup bread crumbs

Directions:
1. Preheat the air fryer to 370 degrees for 2 minutes.
2. Cut the jalapeno peppers in half long ways and take out the seeds. Rinse them out and set aside to drain.
3. Place the cream cheese in a bowl and mix in the parsley with a fork. Also mix in half of the bread crumbs. This is the filling. Put the rest of the bread crumbs in a small bowl.
4. Stuff each half of the peppers with the cream cheese mixture.
5. Turn the peppers upside down and press into the remaining bread crumbs.
6. Spray the basket of the air fryer with nonstick spray and place in as many peppers as will fit in the bottom with the bread crumb side up.
7. Cook for 6 to 8 minutes until the tops are brown and the peppers soft and a slightly charred.
8. Repeat with the rest of the filled peppers.

Hot Chips

Hot chips are not spicy hot, although they can be made that way easily by sprinkling the potato slices with cayenne or paprika but are physically hot. I love hot chips and I serve mine with French onion dip. These are hot potato chips, but you can also make them with sweet potatoes and sprinkle a little brown sugar on top while they are still warm.

Ingredients:
2 medium sized russet potatoes, I leave the skins on but you can peel if you like
½ tablespoon Olive Oil
salt to taste

Directions:
1. Clean and peel the potatoes if you like. Slice them thin. I use a mandolin, but if you don't have one, a sharp knife on a cutting board will do.
2. Soak the slices in cold water 15 minutes and drain. Fill the bowl with more cold water and soak again for 15 minutes and drain well.
3. Spread out some paper towels and dry the slices in them blotting them dry with another paper towel.
4. Place them back in the bowl minus the water and toss with the olive oil and salt.
5. Place a layer in the nonstick sprayed bottom of the air fryer and cook at 390 degrees for about 15 minutes. Check them and if they are still pale, give them a few more minutes. They should be slightly crispy yet pliable when you take them out because they will crisp up more as they cool. They should not be dark brown or black. Keep checking because not all air fryers will take 15 to 20 minutes to cook these chips and some might take longer.

Loaded Potato Skins

These potato skins are delicious and crispy and go over well on game day. I use 5 smaller potatoes and have 10 pieces when I am done. They have the smoky flavor of bacon and the onion flavor of fresh chives.

Ingredients:
5 small potatoes, baked ahead of time and halved
½ cup cooked crumbled bacon
½ cup shredded cheddar cheese
2 tablespoons thin sliced chives
Sour cream

Directions:
1. Scoop most of the potato pulp from the skins and retain it for making mashed potatoes another day. Leave a good amount of the potato pulp around the edges so that the skin will stand up on its own. I use a melon baller and just run it down the center of the potato to remove the pulp.
2. Sprinkle the potato halves equally with the bacon, cheddar cheese and chives.
3. Place as many as can fit into the nonstick sprayed basket of the air fryer.
4. Cook 5 to 7 minutes at 370 degrees F or until the cheese melts and does not turn black.
5. Remove with tongs to a plate and top with a dollop of sour cream.

Mozzarella Sticks

Making your own mozzarella sticks is much healthier than getting frozen ones. You can actually use whole wheat flour and skim mozzarella string cheese strips, so they have less calories and fat. This recipe makes 24 sticks.

Ingredients:
1 10-ounce package part skim mozzarella string cheese
¼ cup whole wheat flour
1 large egg
¼ cup panko bread crumbs
¼ cup regular bread crumbs
½ teaspoon garlic powder
½ teaspoon onion powder
½ teaspoon salt
½ teaspoon paprika

Directions:
1. Cut the cheese sticks in half and put them in a closeable bag in the freezer for 30 minutes to 1 hour. They must be frozen.
2. Line a rimmed baking sheet with parchment paper.
3. Take the frozen cheese sticks from the freezer and put them in a second closeable bag. The first one will have ice crystals on it and should no longer be used. Pour the flour into the bag and shake to cover the sticks with the flour.
4. Whisk the egg in a shallow bowl and set aside.

5. Mix the panko, regular bread crumbs, garlic powder, onion powder, salt and paprika in another bowl and mixt to combine. Set this bowl aside too.
6. Take a flour covered stick from the bag and shake off excess flour. Dip in the egg mixture and then in the breadcrumb mixture. Place them on the parchment covered baking sheet and keep going until they are all coated.
7. Place the whole baking sheet in the freezer for at least 1 hour.
8. Preheat the air fryer to 370 degrees for 4 minutes.
9. Take some of the frozen cheese and place them in a single layer in the basket of the air fryer that is sprayed with nonstick spray. Six should fit nicely. Put the other ones back in the freezer until you are ready to cook them.
10. Cook for 5 to 8 minutes. Start checking at 5. They are done when lightly golden brown and soft.
11. Serve with ranch or marinara dipping sauce.

Parmesan Fried Dills

Fried Dill Pickles? Why not! The pickles are cut into chips and covered with breadcrumbs, Parmesan cheese and dill then fried in the air fryer. This makes a bunch and is appropriate for tailgate parties or sports parties and even for the family. They are really good – Really!

Ingredients:
I 32-ounce jar of whole dill pickles
½ cup panko bread crumbs

¼ cup fresh grated Parmesan Cheese
¼ teaspoon dried dill weed
2 eggs, beaten

Directions:

1. Preheat the air fryer to 400 degrees F for 3 minutes.
2. Remove the pickles from the jar and slice in chips that are about ¼ inch thick. Dry them off between several layers of paper towel.
3. In a closeable plastic bag, mix the bread crumbs, parmesan and dill weed and set aside.
4. In a bowl, beat the eggs.
5. Dip the pickle chips or slices in the egg and shake off any excess. Place them in the bag and shake so they get coated well.
6. Spray the basket of the air fryer with nonstick spray and put in as many pickle slices as will fit without overlapping much.
7. Cook 8 to 10 minutes shaking the basket after about 5 minutes in.
8. Continue cooking the rest of the pickles.
9. Serve with ranch for dip.

Phyllo Encrusted Brie

This is a rather elegant appetizer for a dinner party using puff pastry and brie cheese. The cheese gets all nice and melty inside the pastry and goes nicely with a glass of wine. The recipe makes about 6 servings. You will need a springform pan that fits in an air fryer. I have a 4-inch one that fits with some room around the edges, so a 5-inch one might fit.

Ingredients:

8 sheets phyllo pastry dough, leave out to room temperature
1/3 cup melted butter
8 ounces of round brie cheese wheel
2 tablespoons cranberry jelly (I used whole cranberry sauce with a little sugar mixed in and it worked and I have used raspberry jam and that tasted pretty good)

Directions:

1. Place a sheet of phyllo pastry in the bottom of a nonstick sprayed spring form pan. Press it to mold into the shape of the pan, but you want the ends of the sheets to come up over the side of the pan because you will be moving them down over the top of the brie when you are done.
2. Lightly brush the sheet with melted butter.
3. Put in another sheet of phyllo so that the corners overlap and push into the pan. Brush with melted butter.
4. Continue with the rest of the phyllo sheets and butter
5. Lightly scrape the sides of the brie rind with a vegetable peeler. Place the peels in the middle of the phyllo pastry lined pan and the brie wheel on top.
6. Spread the top of the brie with the cranberry jam or sauce.
7. Carefully fold the phyllo sheets over the brie, one at a time. They will be fragile. Brush with butter so they stick together over top of the brie.
8. Spray the top of the covered brie with a good coating of butter flavored cooking spray.
9. Place the pan in the basket of the air fryer and set for 390 degrees F and check after 10 minutes. The pastry should be brown and the brie should be soft. If it isn't, let it go another 3 to 5 minutes.
10. Carefully remove the spring form pan from the basket and protect your hands. It will be hot. Let it cool a little and remove the sides.
11. Slice in wedges and serve.

Ranch Fried Chick Peas

These little gems are some of my favorite treats. I love chick peas to begin with and when you fry them with ranch, well, it is simply heaven. You use a whole can of chickpeas and Ranch seasoning mix you get in packages. Make Italian flavored chick peas with a package of dry Italian dressing too.

Ingredients:
1 15-ounce can chickpeas, drained but do not rinse them.
2 tablespoons olive oil, divided
1 package dry Ranch dressing mix
1 teaspoon sea salt
2 tablespoons lemon juice

Directions:
1. Drain the chickpeas and put them into a bowl with 1 tablespoon of the olive oil.
2. Spray the inside basket of the air fryer with nonstick cooking spray and pour the chickpeas in. All of them!
3. Set the air fryer for 400 degrees F and air fry for 15 minutes.
4. Pour the hot chickpeas back in the bowl and pour in the rest of the olive oil, the ranch dressing mix, salt and the lemon juice and use a spoon to mix them around so they are coated well.
5. Spray the inside of the basket with nonstick spray and pour all of the chickpeas back in.
6. Set for 350 degrees F for 5 minutes.
7. Cool and store in an airtight container. They are better eaten cold.

Stuffed Fried Chicken Wontons

This recipe makes a whopping 50 appetizers. I usually make some chicken and some pork so I would use ½ pound of each and mix it separately halving everything in the recipe. These are so good even 50 of them aren't going to last very long. They do cook about 10 minutes, so it is best to try and keep the ones you do first warm in a 350 degree F oven covered with foil until they are all finished.

Ingredients:
1 pound ground chicken, beef, pork or white turkey meat
2 cloves garlic, peeled and minced
1 tablespoon fresh ginger, grated
2 tablespoons green onion, chopped fine
2 tablespoons oyster sauce
1 tablespoon soy sauce
2 cups chopped cabbage
1 egg
1 tablespoon water
50 wonton wrappers, 3-inch square ones
olive oil in a spray mist bottle or olive oil flavored cooking spray

Directions:
1. In a large bowl, combine the meat, garlic, ginger, green onion, oyster sauce, soy sauce and cabbage. The mixture is very sticky.

2. Whisk the egg with the water in a small bowl to make an egg wash.
3. Place a wonton wrapper in the palm of one hand and with the index finger of the other hand, dip into the egg wash and paint all 4 edges of the wrapper.
4. Place 1 teaspoon of the filling into the center of the wrapper and fold 1 corner catty-corner to the opposite corner to enclose the filling. Squeeze out any air bubbles and seal around the edges.
5. Place as many of the wontons in the nonstick sprayed basket of the air fryer that will fit in one layer. Spray or mist on a liberal amount of olive oil.
6. Cook at 350 degrees F for 4 minutes.
7. Remove basket and shake the wontons around flipping over as many wontons as you can. Spray again with olive oil and let fry another 4 to 6 minutes or until golden brown.
8. Continue with the rest of the wontons.
9. Serve with duck sauce dip.

Vegetable Spring Rolls

I hate greasy spring rolls. These are far from greasy and are very light. Because they are not greasy, you can taste the flavors of the vegetables inside much better. You will never want to eat a spring roll fried in oil again once you taste one, or two or more, of these. This recipe makes 10 spring rolls

Ingredients:
1 clove garlic, peeled and minced
1 green onion, chopped fine
1 teaspoon fresh grated ginger
1 teaspoon olive oil
½ cup carrot, sliced thin
¼ of a yellow bell pepper, seeded and thin sliced
¼ of a red bell pepper, seeded and thin sliced
5 medium mushrooms, cleaned and sliced thin
½ cup cabbage, sliced thin
1 tablespoon soy sauce
1 tablespoon oyster sauce
10 spring roll wrappers, I use frozen ones

Directions:
1. Sauté the garlic, onion and ginger in a frying pan with 1 teaspoon olive oil (about 2 minutes).
2. Add the carrot and cook 2 minutes.
3. Add the bell peppers, mushrooms and cabbage and sauté. Once the cabbage wilts and mushrooms release their liquid, add the soy sauce and oyster sauce and turn to low. Cook 10 minutes stirring occasionally. Once there is no more liquid in the pan, the vegetables are done. Remove from heat and let cool completely.
4. Remove the spring roll wrappers from the freezer and cover with a clean, damp towel. Leave out 30 minutes while vegetables are cooling.
5. Preheat the air fryer to 380 degrees F for 4 minutes.
6. Place a spring roll sheet on a clean surface so it looks like a diamond shape. Put 1 tablespoon of the mixture about 1 inch from the triangle closes to you and roll up half way. Tuck in the right and left corners and roll all the way up. Make sure you roll them tightly.
7. Place 5 of the spring rolls in the air fryer basket that has been sprayed with olive oil flavored cooking spray. If 5 won't fit in a single layer put in 4. Spray the tops of the spring rolls generously with the cooking spray and cook for 10 minutes.

Stop the air fryer after 5 minutes and shake the rolls so they turn over. Watch after 8 minutes so they don't burn.

8. Repeat with the rest of the wrappers.

Now you have breakfast, lunch and appetizers and snacks under your belt with your air fryer, so let's go on to some main dishes made with poultry.

Chapter 5: Mouthwatering Chicken and Turkey Recipes

This chapter focuses on poultry, especially chicken and turkey, that is simply delicious in the air fryer. I am sure you figured this chapter would contain fried chicken, and it does. There is a recipe for chicken tenders and chicken nuggets too. Other things you may not have been aware of is that you can cook a turkey breast in an air fryer. Caribbean Chicken, BBQ chicken, tandoori chicken and turkey meatballs are also included in this chapter with much more. There are 20 poultry recipes you can try and I guarantee you and your family will love most of them.

Amazing Chicken Parmesan

Chicken Parmesan has a breaded and fried chicken breast served with pasta and sauce. The chicken tends to be a little on the oily side because it is normally deep fried. When you do it in an air fryer, it comes out crispy and light and with less calories. A variation on this recipe is to make the chicken breast, melt the cheese over top, put a little sauce on top and put it in a bun to make chicken parmesan sandwiches. This recipe makes 4 servings.

Ingredients:
2 8-ounce chicken breasts, sliced in half to make 4 thin pieces
2 tablespoons grated Parmesan cheese
6 tablespoons Italian seasoned bread crumbs

1 tablespoon butter, melted
6 tablespoons shredded mozzarella cheese
½ cup marinara sauce

Directions:

1. Preheat the air fryer to 360 degrees F for 9 minutes. You want it to be very hot to begin with.
2. In a bowl, whisk the parmesan and bread crumbs and set aside.
3. Melt the butter in another bowl.
4. Use a brush to brush the butter onto each chicken breast piece and dip into the cheese breadcrumb mixture pressing the breading into the breast (otherwise it will fly around in the air fryer because of the wind it creates).
5. Remove the basket from the air fryer when done preheating and spray with butter or olive oil flavored cooking spray. Place 2 of the breasts in and spray the tops with the cooking spray.
6. Cook 6 minutes. Remove the basket and flip the breasts over. Top each breast with 1 tablespoon of the sauce and 1 ½ tablespoon of the mozzarella.
7. Cook 3 more minutes or until the cheese is melted and brown. I do check my chicken with the ready read meat thermometer to make sure the internal temperature is 165 degrees F.
8. Keep the two breasts warm while cooking the other two.
9. Serve with pasta and more marinara sauce.

Basic BBQ Chicken

This basic BBQ chicken isn't too sweet and it isn't too spicy. The three bears would say it is just right. The marinade is simple to make with things you probably already have in the kitchen with the exception of Chipotle Chili Powder. I have made it with regular chili powder and it works, but the chipotle gives it a little extra flavor. The recipe makes 6 drumsticks.

Ingredients:
2 tablespoons Worcestershire Sauce
1 tablespoon honey
¾ cup ketchup
2 teaspoons chipotle chili powder
6 chicken drumsticks

Directions:
1. Preheat the air fryer to 370 degrees F for 5 minutes.
2. Use a big bowl to mix the Worcestershire sauce, honey, ketchup and chili powder. Whisk it up well.
3. Drop in the drumsticks and turn them so they are all coated with the mixture.
4. Spray the basket of the air fryer with nonstick spray and place 3 chicken drumsticks in.
5. Cook for 17 minutes for large drumsticks 15 minutes for smaller ones, flipping when it reaches half the time.
6. Repeat with the other three drumsticks.

Basic No Frills Turkey Breast

This recipe requires an 8 pound turkey breast with the bone in. It is seasoned simply, so if you like other seasonings, feel free to add them.   This will provide 6 servings.

Ingredients:
1 bone in turkey breast (about 8 pounds)
2 tablespoons olive oil
2 tablespoons sea salt
1 tablespoon black pepper

Directions:
1. Preheat the air fryer to 360 degrees F for about 8 minutes.
2. Rub the washed turkey breast with the olive oil both on the skin and on the inside of the cavity.
3. Sprinkle on the sea salt and black pepper.
4. Remove the basket from the air fryer and spray with butter or olive oil flavored nonstick spray.
5. Put the turkey in with the breast side down.
6. Cook 20 minutes and carefully turn the breast over.
7. Spray with cooking oil and cook another 20 minutes.
8. When done test with thermometer and it should read 165 degrees F. If not, put it back in for a few minutes.
9. Let the breast rest at least 15 minutes before cutting and serving.

Better Than Fast Food Chicken Nuggets

This recipe makes 4 servings of chicken nuggets and you will never want to buy them from a fast food restaurant every again. They are very crunchy outside and moist inside and you will be astounded at the ease it is to cook up a batch. I make a bunch and freeze them. When I need a few, I just pop them into the nonstick sprayed basket of the air fryer frozen and set for 400 degrees F and cook for 6 minutes, flip and cook another 6 minutes.

Ingredients:
2 large skinless, boneless chicken breasts (about 16 ounces)
½ teaspoon sea salt
½ teaspoon black pepper
2 teaspoons olive oil
2 tablespoons panko bread crumbs
6 tablespoons seasoned bread crumbs
2 tablespoon grated Parmesan cheese
Olive oil flavored cooking spray

Directions:
- Preheat the air fryer to 400 degrees F for about 8 minutes.
- Cut the chicken into 1-inch pieces and put them in a bowl seasoning with salt and pepper.

102

- Put the olive oil in the bowl and toss well to coat all the pieces.
- Place the panko crumbs, seasoned crumbs and Parmesan in a bowl.
- Place some of the chicken chunks in the crumb mixture and toss so each nugget is coated.
- Spray the basket with nonstick spray and place about 6 to 8 of the nuggets in, spraying them with the olive oil spray lightly.
- Cook 8 minutes, turning after 4 and spraying again. They should be golden brown when done.
- Repeat with all the chicken chunks and serve with dipping sauce of your choice.

Caribbean Chicken

This chicken will give you a flavor of the Polynesian islands and make you think you are sitting at a luau on watching hula girls and fire dancers. You want to use chicken thighs because they create a moister chicken than breasts would. This recipe makes about 8 6-ounce portions and it will get your taste buds jumping.

Ingredients:
3 pounds boneless, skinless chicken thighs
sea salt to taste
coarse ground black pepper to taste
1 tablespoon cayenne pepper
1 tablespoon coriander seed
1 tablespoon ground cinnamon

1 ½ teaspoons ground nutmeg
1 ½ teaspoons ground ginger
3 tablespoons coconut oil, melted

Directions:

1. Preheat the air fryer to 390 degrees for 5 minutes.
2. Pat the chicken dry and place on a baking sheet covered with paper towels. You want to get rid of most of the liquid from being in the refrigerator, so let sit about 20 minutes before starting to cook.
3. Salt and pepper the chicken and leave sitting on the baking sheet.
4. In a bowl mix up the cayenne, coriander, cinnamon, nutmeg and ginger.
5. Put the chicken pieces in the spice mixture and coat all of them well. Place back on the baking tray that no longer has the paper towels on it.
6. Brush all sides of each thigh with the melted coconut oil with a pastry brush.
7. Put 4 pieces of the chicken in the basket of the air fryer that has been sprayed with nonstick spray. They may overlap slightly.
8. Cook for 10 minutes, flipping after 5 minutes.
9. Repeat with other chicken thighs and keep the first ones warm until they are all done.

Faire-Worthy Turkey Legs

If you have ever been to a Renaissance Faire, you know that turkey legs are a favorite food that you can get there. These rival the deliciousness of those turkey legs. What I like is that the legs are a little bit crispy on the outside and deliciously moist on the inside. They don't take much to make either. This recipe makes 1 turkey leg so you will have to have 4 times the ingredients if you are making four of them and you will have to cook them separately.

Ingredients:

I turkey leg
1 teaspoon olive oil
1 teaspoon poultry seasoning
1 teaspoon garlic powder
¼ teaspoon salt
1 pinch black pepper

Directions:

1. Preheat the air fryer to 350 degrees F for about 4 minutes.
2. Coat the leg with the olive oil. Just use your hands and rub it in.
3. In a small bowl, mix the poultry seasoning, garlic powder, salt and pepper. Rub it on the turkey leg.
4. Coat the inside of the air fryer basket with nonstick spray and place the turkey leg in.
5. Cook for 27 minutes, turning at 14 minutes. Be sure the leg is done by inserting a meat thermometer in the fleshy part of the leg and it should read 165 degrees F.

Feta and Spinach Stuffed Chicken Breast

Serve this meal to guests because it is very elegant and tasty. The outside is crispy with juicy chicken and creamy cheese and spinach inside. I like to serve it with garlicy green beans or some chopped zucchini, summer squash and tomatoes cooked with some herbs and spices. It makes 4 servings.

Ingredients:

2 tablespoons olive oil, divided
1 small onion, peeled and chopped
1 clove garlic, peeled and minced
4 cups packed baby spinach, chopped
Salt and pepper to taste
¼ cup feta or goat cheese, crumbled
4 whole boneless, skinless chicken breasts
2 eggs
½ cup all-purpose flour or almond flour
1/4 teaspoon garlic powder
¼ teaspoon paprika
¼ teaspoon sea salt
1/8 teaspoon pepper

Directions:

1. Place 1 tablespoon of the olive oil in a hot skillet and add the onions. Sauté for 2 to 3 minutes over medium heat. Add the garlic and sauté 1 or 2 more minutes.

2. Add the spinach, a little salt and pepper to taste and cook until the spinach wilts. Transfer to a mixing bowl to cool with a slotted spoon so the amount of juice from the spinach is minimal.
3. Once the mixture cools, drain out the liquid that is left.
4. Add the feta or goat cheese to the bowl and mix it up. Set the bowl aside while you prepare the chicken.
5. Cut ¾ of the way through each breast to create a pocket. Avoid cutting all the way through.
6. Sprinkle the inside of the chicken with a little salt and pepper and put 2 tablespoons of the spinach mix inside.
7. Preheat the air fryer to 400 degrees F for 4 to 5 minutes.
8. While preheating, whisk the eggs in a shallow bowl.
9. In another bowl, whisk together the flour, garlic powder, paprika, salt and pepper.
10. Dip one chicken breast in the flour mixture. Shake off excess and dip into the eggs and then back in the flour mixture again. Set on a tray and do the other chicken breasts.
11. Brush the chicken breasts with the remaining olive oil using a pastry brush. (I have also used a mister with olive oil in it and that worked well).
12. Spray nonstick spray on the basket of the air fryer and lay the chicken with the oiled side down inside the basket oiling or spraying the other side as well. You may be able to get two of the breasts in at a time.
13. Cook 10 minutes, flip and cook another 10 minutes. Check with a meat thermometer to make sure the internal temperature is 165 degrees F.
14. Remove from air fryer and keep warm until the other two breasts are finished and serve.

Garlic Flavored Parmesan Chicken Tenders

My nephews love these chicken tenders because they are so crunchy and delicious. I season them with parmesan to give them a little kick and add onion and garlic powder with the regular salt and pepper. You will have 3 bowls out when you go to bread the tenders. One is for flour and I have used whole wheat flour before and it worked well, but I prefer the all-purpose flour. The next bowl is for your egg wash and the last bowl for the breadcrumbs, herb and cheese mixture. Serve it with dipping sauce. I used bottled BBQ, Ranch dressing and honey.

Ingredients:
¼ cup flour
1 egg
2 tablespoons water
1 cup panko bread crumbs
1 teaspoon garlic powder
1 teaspoon onion powder
¼ teaspoon sea salt
¼ teaspoon ground black pepper
¼ cup grated, fresh Parmesan cheese
8 skinless chicken tenders
Butter flavor cooking spray

Directions:

1. Prepare the three bowls. Place flour in one, whisk egg and water in another and combine the bread crumbs, garlic powder, onion, salt, pepper and Parmesan cheese in the last bowl.
2. Preheat the air fryer to 400 degrees F for 5 minutes
3. Pat the chicken with paper towels to get some of the moisture off.
4. Dredge lightly in the flour and then in the egg mixture.
5. Dredge in the bread crumb mixture and press the mixture into the chicken so it won't fly off when the high powered wind comes through the air fryer.
6. Spray the basket of the air fryer with the cooking spray and place 3 or 4 of the tenders (as many you can get in there with them overlapping) in the bottom. Spray liberally with the butter flavor cooking spray on tops of the tenders.
7. Cook 6 minutes, pause the air fryer and flip, and cook another 6 minutes after spraying the other side of the chicken with the butter flavored cooking spray.
8. Repeat with the rest of the chicken tenders and serve with dip.

General Tso's Chicken

General Tso's Chicken is a spicy Asian dish where the chicken is fried and covered with a hot and delicious sauce. The recipe calls for six dried red chilis, but I don't like mine quite so hot, so I only use three. This recipe coats the chicken in potato starch instead of flour and I honestly like it much better because it is a little lighter than flour. Find potato starch at a whole food store if you can't get it in your super market. This recipe makes 4 servings

Ingredients:
2 pounds chicken thighs, boneless and skinless
1/3 cup potato starch
1 tablespoon vegetable oil
3 green onions
2 tablespoons garlic, minced
6 dried red chilies
1 teaspoon fresh ginger, minced
¾ cup brown sugar
½ cup soy sauce
½ cup chicken broth
2 tablespoons rice vinegar
1 teaspoon sesame oil
1/8 teaspoon salt
¼ cup water (optional)
2 teaspoons cornstarch (optional)

Directions:
1. Preheat the air fryer to 400 degrees F for 5 minutes.
2. Cut the chicken in 1-inch pieces and place in a bowl with the potato starch. Toss to make sure each piece is coated.
3. Place the chicken pieces in the air fryer making sure not to overlap. I use silicon coated tongs to do this.
4. Spray with a little butter flavored nonstick spray and shake the basket before putting it into the air fryer.
5. Cook 20 minutes removing and shaking the basket every 5 minutes. The chicken is brown and crispy when done.
6. Repeat with rest of the chicken pieces and keep everything warm in a 350 degree oven covered with foil.
7. Make the sauce by heating the vegetable oil in a skillet over medium high heat and add the onions, garlic, red chilies, and ginger. Sauté for 1 or 2 minutes until the chilies start to turn bright red and the onions soften.

8. In a bowl, mix the brown sugar, soy sauce, chicken broth, rice vinegar, sesame oil and a pinch of salt. Whisk well and pour it into the skillet and bring to a boil. Let it simmer for about 3 minutes.
9. Place the chicken pieces in a high rimmed platter.
10. If the sauce is not thick enough for you, dissolve the cornstarch in the water and add to the sauce. Bring it back to a boil and let it cook, stirring constantly, until thickened.
11. Pour the sauce over the chicken and serve with rice.

Grandma's Fried Chicken Without All The Grease

You can have fried chicken again with just a fraction of the grease. This recipe might taste better than grandma's chicken and calories and fat are greatly reduced. This makes 4 chicken thighs and chicken thighs are used because they fit better in an air fryer. You can do breasts too but you must cook them a little longer and only do 1 at a time. The ingredients shown work for 4 thighs or 2 breasts all bone in.

Ingredients:
½ cup all-purpose flour
½ teaspoon garlic powder
½ teaspoon onion powder
¼ teaspoon sea salt
¼ teaspoon ground black pepper

1 tablespoon Old Bay Cajun Seasoning (optional)
1 egg
1 tablespoon water
4 chicken thighs

Directions:

1. Preheat the air fryer to 390 degrees for 5 minutes.
2. Prepare a bowl by whisking the flour, garlic powder, onion powder, sea salt, pepper and old bay seasoning all together. I use a deep dish pie plate.
3. Whisk the egg and water together in a bowl.
4. Pat the chicken dry with paper towels and dredge in the flour mixture.
5. Dip in the egg mixture and then back in the flour mixture. Shake off any excess flour.
6. Spray the basket of the air fryer with butter flavored cooking spray and put the chicken thighs in the bottom.
7. Cook for 25 minutes or until internal temperature gets to 180 degrees F.
8. Serve with some mashed potatoes, biscuits and green beans.

Herb Air Fried Chicken Thighs

These herb rubbed chicken thighs are very delicious and they are simple to make. They have the taste of thyme, rosemary and lemon and make for a wonderful family dinner. This is enough for 2 big eaters and 4 petite eaters.

Ingredients:

2 pounds deboned chicken thighs

1 teaspoon rosemary

1 teaspoon thyme

1 teaspoon garlic powder

½ teaspoon lemon pepper

1 large lemon

Directions:

1. Trim fat from thighs and salt and pepper all sides.
2. In a small bowl, combine the rosemary, thyme, garlic powder and lemon pepper. Sprinkle over the chicken thighs and press the mixture in putting them on a baking sheet.
3. Cut the lemon and squeeze the juice over all the chicken thighs. Cover with plastic wrap and put in the refrigerator for 30 minutes.
4. Preheat the air fryer to 360 degrees F for 6 minutes and spray with butter flavored cooking spray.
5. Place the thighs in the air fryer basket, as many will fit in one layer.
6. Cook for 15 minutes, turning after 7 minutes. Check internal temperature to make sure it is at 180 degrees F before serving.

Herb Butter and Bacon Roasted Turkey Breast

I love the flavor of fresh herbs on my turkey and all the herbs in this recipe should be fresh and not dried. You can usually find sage, rosemary, oregano and thyme in the grocery store. You use a 6 pound turkey breast, give a ½ pound or so) and it serves 8 people. Believe it or not, you can do a slow cook in an air fryer by keeping the temperature low. It produces a turkey that is super moist and flavorful with just a little bit of crispness on the outside.

Ingredients:
3 tablespoons unsalted butter, room temperature
1 tablespoon oregano, finely chopped
1 tablespoon sage leaves, finely chopped
1 tablespoon thyme leaves, finely chopped
1 tablespoon rosemary leaves, finely chopped
3 slices cooked and crumbled bacon
1 6-pound turkey breast, rinsed and dried
1 teaspoon kosher salt
1 teaspoon black pepper

Directions:
1. Make the herb butter by mixing the butter, oregano, sage, thyme, rosemary and bacon well. I use a fork and then switch to a spoon and use the back to get it mixed in. Place a piece of parchment paper on a flat surface and scrape the butter into the middle of it. Roll the parchment up into a log of butter and secure the paper with tape. Put the log into the freezer until the turkey is done.
2. Sprinkle the salt and pepper over the turkey breast on all sides. Rub it in.
3. Spray the basket of the air fryer with nonstick spray and place the breast in the basket.
4. Set for 300 degrees F and time for 1 hour. When the alarm goes off, set the heat to 270 degrees F and cook another 15 minutes or until the internal temperature reaches 165 degrees F.

5. Remove basket from the air fryer and let cool 15 minutes. At this time, take the butter out of the freezer. You don't want it to completely thaw, it must be a little bit hard to cut slices.
6. Cut the meat from the bones and place a pat of the herb butter on top so it melts over the turkey.

Left Over Turkey Croquets

I don't know about you, but I always have left over turkey at Thanksgiving and it is usually more than I can stomach at one time. I do not like the texture turkey gets when it is frozen, so I make all kinds of recipes out of leftover turkey. This one works well in the air fryer. Turkey Croquets are little balls of goodness that are crispy on the outside and light and flavorful on the inside. In the air fryer they do not get oil laden and are healthier for you. Not only do you use leftover turkey, but also left over stuffing and left over gravy, not to mention the cranberry sauce. It makes 12 croquets, which is enough for dinner for 1 or 2 people.

Ingredients:
½ cup flour
2 large eggs, beaten
1 cup Panko bread crumbs
1/8 teaspoon salt
1/8 teaspoon pepper
olive oil in a mister
2 cups leftover stuffing
1 cup chopped turkey meat
1 cup turkey gravy, warmed
½ cup cranberry sauce

Directions:
1. Place the flour in a shallow bowl and set it aside.
2. Beat the eggs in another bowl and set it aside.
3. Mix the bread crumbs, salt and pepper in another bowl and set it aside.
4. Preheat the air fryer to 380 degrees for 4 minutes.
5. Take a golf ball-sized amount of the stuffing and put it in your palm. Take about 2 teaspoons of the turkey and put it in the

middle of the stuffing and squeeze the stuffing around the turkey so you have a stuffing ball that has turkey in the middle.

6. Coat the ball in the flour and make sure there is a light coating all over it.
7. Dip it into the egg and coat well.
8. Press in the Panko mixture so it stays put in the air fryers.
9. Spray the basket of the air fryer with a good coating of olive oil and put in as many of the balls as you can without them overlapping. You don't want them touching because they won't brown evenly if they do. I was able to get 5 or 6 in at a time.
10. Spray the croquets (balls) liberally with the olive oil and cook for 6 minutes. Roll the croquets over and spray again, cooking them for 4 more minutes. It might take more or less time depending on your air fryer so keep an eye on them.
11. While the croquets are cooking, heat up the turkey gravy and put it in a small bowl. Place the cranberry sauce in another bowl and use both for a dip.

Lemon Fried Chicken

This dish is lemony fresh and crunchy because you use corn meal to bread the chicken. I use 2 large chicken breasts that are boneless and skinless and press down and slice through sideways so I have 2 pieces of breast that look like thinner chicken breasts. You can only put two of them in the air fryer at a time, so you must put the done ones in the oven at 350 covered with foil to keep them warm while the other two cook. I serve with lemon flavored couscous with peas and almonds cooked in and then make green beans with lemon butter to serve on the side. This recipe makes 4 servings of chicken.

Ingredients:
¼ cup flour
1 large egg, beaten
Juice of 1 lemon
½ cup corn meal
¾ teaspoon garlic powder
2 teaspoons fresh thyme, finely chopped
¾ teaspoon paprika
2 tablespoons fresh lemon zest (from the lemon you juiced. Get the zest first and set aside)
½ teaspoon salt
¼ teaspoon pepper
2 large chicken breasts, cut in half
Olive oil or butter flavored cooking spray

Directions:
1. Place the flour in a shallow bowl, like a deep dish pie plate and set it aside.
2. Whisk the egg in a bowl and add the juice of the lemon. Whisk well and set the bowl aside.
3. In another shallow plate, whisk together the corn meal, garlic powder, thyme, paprika, lemon zest, salt and pepper and set it aside.
4. Preheat the air fryer to 400 degrees F for 5 minutes.
5. Lightly salt and pepper the breasts on both sides to taste.
6. Dip in the flour and make sure it is totally covered with a light coating.
7. Shake off excess and dip in the egg mixture.
8. Place the breast in the cornmeal mixture and press in on all sides so it is totally encrusted.
9. Spray the basket with nonstick cooking spray and place 2 of the breasts in the basket spraying the tops of them liberally with the spray.
10. Cook for 10 minutes and pull out the basket and turn the breasts spraying the top with the cooking spray. Cook another

10 minutes.   Always check internal temperature before removing from the air fryer.
11. Repeat with other two breasts while keeping the ones just cooked hot.

Roasted Whole Chicken in an Air Fryer

If you can get a turkey breast in an air fryer, you should be able to get a whole chicken in and roast it to perfection. A 4.5 pound chicken fits pretty good with the breast end down and legs near the lid. You are pushing it at 5 pounds. It will definitely be snug because of the thighs and legs. Don't let that deter you from trying to do it because the results are astoundingly good.

Ingredients:
2 teaspoons sea salt
1 teaspoon garlic powder
1 teaspoon onion powder
1 teaspoon paprika
½ teaspoon pepper
½ teaspoon dried thyme
½ teaspoon dried rosemary
½ teaspoon dried parsley
½ teaspoon dry mustard
1 (4 to 5 pound) whole chicken
butter flavor cooking oil

Directions:

1. Preheat the air fryer to 350 degrees 8 minutes.
2. In a small bowl, whisk the salt, garlic powder, onion powder, paprika, pepper, thyme, rosemary, parsley and mustard.
3. Wash out the chicken and dry inside and out with a paper towel.
4. Rub the herb mix into the outside of the chicken and in the inside of the cavity.
5. Spray the preheated air fryer basket with butter flavor spray and put the chicken in breast side down.   Spray the chicken with the cooking spray.
6. Cook 30 minutes and carefully turn the chicken over. Spray with nonstick spray and cook another 30 minutes. Check with a thermometer to make sure it is done to 165 degrees F.   A five pound chicken might take 35 minutes on each side.
7. Remove chicken to a cutting board and let it rest 10 minutes before carving.

Salt and Pepper Wings

These little wings only have 3 ingredients but they are truly tasty. The salt and pepper enhance the flavor of the chicken without the aid of anything else and the wings are crispy and savory. The recipe makes 4 servings and uses 2 pounds of wings. I like the drumettes or wingettes.

Ingredients:

2 teaspoons salt
2 teaspoons fresh ground pepper
2 pounds chicken wings

Directions:
1. In a large bowl combine the salt and pepper.
2. Add the wings to the bowl and mix with your hands to coat every last one.
3. Put 8 to 10 wings in the basket that has been sprayed with nonstick cooking spray. Set for 350 degrees F (there is no need to preheat) and cook about 15 minutes, turning once at 7 minutes.
4. Repeat with rest of wings and serve hot.

Southwestern Style Chicken

When you say southwestern style, you immediately think of something packed with flavor and probably a punch. This recipe does have cumin and chili powder in it but there are no jalapenos waiting to take your breath away. The chicken is very flavorful but it does not have a lot of heat and I like it that way. Give those that want that punch of heat some hot sauce to sprinkle over the chicken if they want. Avoid using fat chicken breasts, but if that is all you can find, cut them in half and still have enough for a serving. This recipe makes 4 servings.

Ingredients:
1 pound skinless, boneless chicken breasts, thawed if frozen
2 tablespoons fresh lime juice
1 tablespoon avocado oil
¼ teaspoon garlic powder
¼ teaspoon onion powder
¼ teaspoon chili powder
¼ teaspoon salt
½ teaspoon cumin

Directions:

1. Place the chicken into a gallon sized closeable bag and pour in the lime juice and the avocado oil. Seal and shake so that the breasts become coated.
2. In a bowl, combine the chili powder, cumin, onion powder, garlic powder and salt. Pour that into the bag with the chicken and squeeze and shake to mix it up.
3. Let the bag sit in the refrigerator 10 minutes.
4. After 5 minutes has elapsed, preheat the air fryer to 400 degrees F for 5 minutes.
5. Place the chicken in a nonstick spray treated air fryer basket and cook for 17 minutes, flipping and spraying again, and cooking another 12 minutes. You will have to do this in batches.
6. Check to make sure the breasts reach 165 degrees F internal temperature before serving.

Sweet Mustard Glazed Turkey Breast

Hope there is enough left over to make a sandwich because there might not be. I will slice my turkey breast away from the table and hid a few slices for sandwiches to take to work one day. This recipe calls for a 5 pound bone in turkey breast and that will be snug in your air fryer so do not get it any bigger. I have been able to stuff and 5.5 pound one in, but no bigger. Do not use any type of syrup except real maple syrup. The stuff you get in the grocery store does not do this recipe justice. This will serve 6 people.

Ingredients:

2 teaspoons olive oil
1 5-pound turkey breast
1 teaspoon salt
1 teaspoon dried thyme
½ teaspoon paprika
½ teaspoon dried sage
½ teaspoon ground pepper
2 tablespoons Dijon mustard
¼ cup maple syrup
1 tablespoon butter

Directions:

1. Preheat the air fryer to 350 degrees F for 8 minutes.
2. Wash and rinse your turkey breast and pat it dry with paper towels.
3. Brush the olive oil all over the breast. I use my hands and even get some inside the cavity (you might need a little more)
4. In a bowl, combine the salt, thyme, paprika, sage and pepper and whisk to combine well.
5. Rub the turkey breast with this herb rub on the outside and make sure it is all generously covered.
6. Spray the air fryer basket with nonstick butter flavored spray and put the turkey in, breast side down. Cook 25 minutes.
7. Carefully turn the turkey and cook another 12 minutes.
8. While it is cooking, place the Dijon, butter and maple syrup in a saucepan over medium heat and cook until bubbly and well combined.
9. When turkey is done, make sure it is the breast up position and brush the glaze on it liberally. Put it back in and cook 5 more minutes until the turkey is crispy and brown. Let it rest with foil on top of it 5 minutes, remove from the air fryer basket and slice.

Tandoori Style Chicken

This is an ancient food from India cooked in a special cone shaped oven. The air fryer is kind of cone shaped, at least some of them are, but they are quite different than their clay counterparts. Tandoori chicken is marinated in a yogurt marinade and cooked with exotic spices like turmeric and garam masala. I have had chicken cooked in a tandoor and this tastes remarkably similar although not quite the same. It is very good, especially if you like Indian food and this recipe makes 4 deliciously spicy servings.

Ingredients:
¼ cup Greek yogurt
1 tablespoon garlic, minced
1 tablespoon fresh ginger, minced
¼ cup cilantro, chopped
½ teaspoon cayenne pepper
1 teaspoon garam masala
1 teaspoon turmeric
1 teaspoon paprika
½ teaspoon salt
1 pound chicken tenders, cut in half
1 tablespoon ghee or olive oil
2 teaspoons lemon juice
cilantro for garnish

Directions:

1. Use only a glass bowl to mix the ingredients. A metal bowl can cause a chemical reaction between the spices that will not be flavorful. Mix the yogurt, garlic, ginger, cilantro, cayenne, garam masala, turmeric, paprika and salt in the bowl. Whisk it well until creamy and colorful.
2. Add the chicken, cover with a plate and set aside. Do not put in the refrigerator.
3. In 25 minutes, turn on the air fryer to 350 degrees F for 5 minutes to preheat it.
4. Open the air fryer and spray the basket with nonstick cooking spray.
5. Take the chicken and shake off any excess marinade and place in the basket. Only put in enough to make a single layer. You will have to make this in batches.
6. Baste the chicken with the ghee or olive oil brushing it on with a silicone brush on the top.
7. Cook for 10 minutes, flip the chicken over, baste with oil on the other side and cook another 5 to 10 minutes or until the internal temperature of the chicken reaches 165 degrees F.
8. Keep the chicken warm until the rest is finished.
9. Place chicken on a serving plate, squeeze the lemon over top and sprinkle with extra cilantro.

Versatile Turkey Meatballs

These meatballs are deliciously versatile. Make spaghetti and sauce to go with them or put them in a meatball sandwich with more sauce. My favorite way to serve them is with zucchini noodles and sauce. They are very good with an Alfredo sauce too. They come out firm and a little crisp on the outside and moist on the inside. Sometimes turkey meatballs can be a little dry, but when you cook them in an air fryer they stay moist. This recipe makes enough meatballs for 4 people (about 20 meatballs).

Ingredients:
½ cup plain bread crumbs – Do not use Panko because they get too crunchy
1 teaspoon onion powder
1 teaspoon garlic powder
1 teaspoon Italian seasoning
¼ teaspoon salt
¼ teaspoon pepper
¼ cup parmesan cheese
2 eggs, beaten
1 pound ground turkey
olive oil flavored cooking spray

Directions:
1. In a bowl mix the bread crumbs, onion powder, garlic powder, Italian seasoning, salt, pepper and Parmesan cheese. Whisk together well.
2. Crack 2 eggs into the bowl and mix in with the rest of the ingredients.
3. Add the turkey and use your hands to combine well. If the mix is too soggy, add a little more bread crumbs until the mixture holds together when squished together.
4. Preheat the air fryer to 400 degrees F for 5 minutes while you form the meatballs.
5. Scoop out a tablespoon full of the mixture and roll into a ball. Put them on a baking sheet while you make all of them.
6. Spray the basket of the air fryer with cooking spray and place as many meatballs as you can to make a single layer.
7. Cook 6 minutes, remove the basket and shake to flip the meatballs and cook another 6 to 8 minutes or until the meatballs are golden brown.

8. Serve with sauce and pasta or in a bun with sauce and some shredded mozzarella that should melt by itself.

Have a hankering for sea food or fish. That is great because both cook up nicely in an air fryer and the next chapter is chock full of recipes for you to try.

Chapter 6: Seafood Fit For Royalty

When I say you can almost make anything in an air fryer, I am not kidding. It is not possible to make soups or stews, of course, but you can make all kinds of fish and seafood recipes like lobster tail and salmon. Remember that not everything comes out crunchy in an air fryer. It depends on what you put in, but everything that comes out is browned and tasty. Let us start out with some lobster tail and work through scallops, cat fish, shrimp, clams and more.

Air Fryer Lobster Tail

I use frozen lobster tails that have been thawed for this recipe but you can use fresh. Either way you must have muscle to make them because separating the shell from the meat is sometimes difficult. There isn't much to this recipe except butter, salt and pepper but it is so good and so easy you will want to make them for more than just a special occasion. This recipe makes 4 servings.

Ingredients:
4 lobster tails
2 tablespoons butter, melted
½ teaspoon salt
¼ teaspoon pepper

Directions:

1. Preheat the air fryer to 380 degrees F for 5 minutes.
2. Use kitchen shears to cut the lobster through the tail section. Break it (be careful, the shell is sharp) and pull the shell back to expose the meat inside.
3. Brush the tails with melted butter and season with salt and pepper. You should have butter left over.
4. Spray the air fryer basket with nonstick cooking spray and if you can get them all in the basket without overlapping them, do so. If not, do them in batches of 2 and watch the time. It might not take as long to cook with less in the air fryer.
5. Cook for 4 minutes, open the air fryer, brush with more butter (use it all this time) and cook for 2 more minutes.
6. Remove them with tongs and serve with more melted butter on the side.

Asian Fried Shrimp With Incredible Sauce

What makes these shrimp Asian is the sweet and spicy sauce you make to go with them. The sauce is called Yum Yum sauce and it is aptly named since it is so yummy. Cut out a piece of parchment to fit in the bottom of your air fryer. Mine is about 8 inches in diameter, so I cut an 8 inch circle and put it in. I then coated it with some nonstick spray and also coated the sides of the basket with it. I then put some of the shrimp on the bottom and propped more around the sides of the basket with the tails up. This allowed me to get more in the basket and not have to do 2 batches. It worked fine. The first time I did not use the nonstick spray or parchment and everything stuck.

Ingredients:

1 tablespoon butter, room temperature
1/3 cup mayonnaise
1 tablespoon rice vinegar
1 tablespoon chili garlic sauce
1 teaspoon paprika
1 teaspoon toasted sesame oil
1 tablespoon brown sugar, pack it well
2 tablespoons cornstarch

¼ teaspoon salt
1 egg
½ cup panko bread crumbs
½ pound shrimp, peeled and deveined with tails still on
1 tablespoon fresh cilantro, chopped

Directions:

1. Place the butter, mayonnaise, rice vinegar and chili garlic sauce in a medium bowl and whip it so it is well combined. Add the paprika, sesame oil and brown sugar and mix it well so there are no lumps. Cover and put it in the refrigerator. This is the yum yum sauce.
2. Prepare the air fryer basket with parchment paper and nonstick cooking spray.
3. In a shallow bowl or pie pan combine the cornstarch and salt.
4. In another dish, beat the egg until frothy.
5. Pour the panko bread crumbs in another shallow dish.
6. Hold shrimp by the tail and dredge in the cornstarch mixture, dip in the egg and throw it into panko bread crumbs and roll it pressing the crumbs in so they stick.
7. Do not preheat the air fryer. Place the shrimp on the bottom on the parchment and prop up on the sides against the basket with tails up.
8. Cook at 350 degrees F for 4 minutes and stop.
9. Pull out the basket and carefully turn the shrimp on the bottom with tongs, then turn the ones on the side as well.
10. Turn the air fryer to 400 degrees F and cook 3 to 5 minutes or until the shrimp is pink and no longer grey or white.
11. Serve with the cold yum yum sauce sprinkled with the cilantro.

Breaded Sea Scallops

Breaded sea scallops make for a great dinner. They only take about 5 to 6 minutes to cook, so if you must do batches, it is still possible to cook and serve. You will need about 18 sea scallops and it is enough for 3 dinner servings, but you can also serve as an appetizer.

Ingredients:
¼ c flour
½ teaspoon paprika
½ teaspoon salt
1/8 teaspoon ground pepper
1 egg
1 ½ tablespoon 2% milk
½ cup corn flake crumbs
Butter flavored cooking spray
18 seas scallops

Directions:
1. In one bowl combine the flour, paprika, salt and pepper and set the bowl aside.
2. In another bowl beat the egg and combine with the milk and set the bowl aside.
3. Take the corn flakes and place between two sheets of wax paper and use a rolling pin to crush them. Put the resulting crumbs in another bowl.

4. Use a paper towel to dry off the scallops and dip individually into the flour mixture, into the egg and milk mixture and finally in the cornflakes making sure to press the flakes in so they stick.
5. Place all the finished scallops on a baking sheet and spray with butter flavored spray, flip and spray the other side.
6. Spray the air fryer with butter flavor spray and put in as many scallops as you can so they do not overlap.
7. Do not preheat the air fryer. Place as many of the scallops in the air fryer basket without overlapping them.
8. Set the air fryer to 400 degrees F and cook 3 minutes, open and flip them over, and cook another 2 to 3 minutes until brown.
9. No matter how much you dry the scallops they will retain water and it will come out after cooking. Place them on a paper towel and let them sit about 1 or 2 minutes and serve with cocktail sauce.

Caramelized Sea Scallops

Caramelized sea scallops are supposed to be browned to a delicious looking caramel color. Unfortunately, they won't get that color in an air fryer, but the upside is, they never overcook and get rubbery. This doesn't take much to make, you need the scallops, oil and salt and pepper. That is it. I use the large variety scallops. You will notice there are no measurements with the ingredients. do as many scallops as you like (I serve 2 of the big ones for a dinner entre).

Ingredients:
Olive oil
Large Sea Scallops
salt and pepper to taste
Butter flavor cooking spray

Directions:
1. Preheat the air fryer to 200 degrees F for 3 minutes.
2. Rub some olive oil in your hands and then rub the scallop with it front and back. Be generous but don't put so much on it drips off easily.
3. Season both sides with salt and pepper to taste.
4. Put 1 or 2 scallops in the nonstick sprayed basket of the air fryer and set the time for 3 minutes.
5. Flip them over and cook another 2 minutes.
6. The scallops will be a little wet so put them on a paper towel for a few minutes and serve.

Coconut Shrimp Air Fryer Style

This recipe will give you a taste of Polynesia with the coconut flavor. You only use egg whites and 1 cup is about 5 or 6 eggs. The yolks make the dip heavy and color the shrimp and you don't want either one. I mix up some crushed pineapple with a bit of Greek yogurt and add a little of the coconut and a tiny bit of sugar, or you can spoon about a half jar of apricot preserves in a sauce pan and heat it up. This creates 12 large shrimp.

Ingredients
12 large raw shrimp, peeled and deveined
1 tablespoon cornstarch
1 cup all-purpose flour
1 cup egg whites only, save the yolks for something else.
1 cup panko bread crumbs
½ teaspoon salt
1 cup unsweetened, dried, shredded coconut

Directions:
1. Place the shrimp on paper towels to dry them off. Let them sit about 5 to 10 minutes.
2. Preheat the air fryer to 350 degrees F for about 5 minutes.
3. Combine the cornstarch and the flour in a shallow dish and mix with a whisk. Set the dish aside.
4. Whisk the egg whites in a bowl and set aside.
5. In another shallow bowl, mix together the panko bread crumbs, salt and coconut and set the dish aside.
6. Take a bunch of paper towels and dry off the tops of the shrimp.
7. Take each one and dredge it into the flour mixture, then dip in the egg whites and toss into the panko/coconut mixture and press in so it sticks to the shrimp.
8. Spray the air fryer basket with cooking spray and place the shrimp in. Do not overlap, you may have to do it in batches.
9. Set for 5 minutes, turn and cook for another 5 minutes.
10. Repeat with the rest of the shrimp.

Crispy Air Fryer Fried Fish

Fish in the air fryer comes out nice and golden crispy on the outside and moist and flaky on the inside. I usually use white fish fillets for this recipe and cut them in half. You do need olive oil in a mist bottle because the cooking spray doesn't get it as crispy. This recipe will serve 4 people.

Ingredients:
¼ cup all-purpose flour
¾ cup fine cornmeal (find in the Latin American section of the grocery store or run it through a blender)
1 teaspoon salt
1 teaspoon paprika
2 teaspoons Old Bay Seasoning
½ teaspoon garlic powder
½ teaspoon onion powder
¼ teaspoon black pepper
4 to 6 white fish fillets cut in half
olive oil in a mist bottle

Directions:
1. Mix the flour, cornmeal, salt, paprika, Old Bay, garlic powder, onion powder and black pepper in a closeable plastic bag and shake.
2. Rinse of the fish fillets and pat them dry with a paper towel leaving them slightly damp.

134

3. One by one place the fillets in the bag with the seasoning and shake until they are completely coated.
4. Spray the basket of the air fryer with cooking spray so the fish won't stick.
5. Place as many fillets in as will fit without laying on top of one another in the basket and mist with the olive oil.
6. Cook 400 degrees F for 10 minutes.
7. Flip the fish over and spray with the olive oil.
8. Cook 7 more minutes. The fish is done when brown and crispy. Watch that it does not turn black and burn. Cooking time depends on the thickness of the fish and it might take less or more time.

Easy and Delicious Air Fried Shrimp

This is another fried shrimp recipe that is a little different because there is ginger in this one. Use fresh ginger that looks like fingers and a hand. Just peel off the out rind and grate the inner flesh. You can use dried ginger too, but it doesn't quite taste as good. This should serve 2 to 3 people.

Ingredients:
2 eggs, beaten
½ cup Panko bread crumbs
1 teaspoon onion powder
1 teaspoon garlic powder
1 teaspoon fresh grated ginger

½ teaspoon salt
¼ teaspoon black pepper
1 pound peeled deveined shrimp

Directions:
1. Preheat the air fryer to 350 degrees for 5 minutes.
2. Beat the eggs in a bowl and set aside.
3. In a deep dish pie plate combine the panko, onion powder, garlic powder, ginger, salt and pepper and mix well.
4. Place the shrimp on paper towels and dab with another paper towel to remove some moisture.
5. Dip each shrimp in the egg and then in the Panko mixture.
6. Spray the basket with cooking spray and place as many shrimp in that will fit and not overlap.
7. Cook 10 minutes, flip the shrimp over and start checking at 7 minutes. It might take until 10 minutes for them to turn pink and be done.

Fish Nuggets

Just like chicken nuggets, kids like fish nuggets and so do some adults. I make these out of cod and they are always a favorite at my house. They are super crispy on the outside and flaky on the inside and I serve them with a tartar sauce dip although my nephew likes them with catsup. This recipe makes about 8 nuggets.

Ingredients:

1 cup cracker crumbs
1 tablespoon olive or vegetable oil
½ cup all-purpose flour
1 egg
1 tablespoon water
salt and pepper to taste
1 to 1 ½ pound cod fillets cut in 8 chunks

Directions:

1. Place the crackers in a food processor and pulse to make fine crumbs.
2. Add the olive oil and process again. Pour the mixture into a shallow dish and set it aside.
3. Pour the flour into a pie plate and set it aside.
4. Whisk the egg with the water in a bowl and set it aside.
5. Salt and pepper each fish nugget and dredge it in the flour. Shake off excess.
6. Dip each nugget in the egg mixture and place it directly into the cracker mixture and press the crumbs in to the nugget.
7. Preheat the air fryer to 350 degrees F.
8. Spray the basket with a cooking spray and place the nuggets in. You will probably have to do this in 2 batches, do not let the nuggets overlap.
9. Set for 7 minutes, turn the nuggets and cook another 8 minutes or until brown and crispy on the outside.

Fish Tacos with Creamy and Delicious Slaw

These are the best fish tacos hands down and that is because the air fryer makes the fish crispy but moist. You make the fish and then put it in a flour tortilla filled with an apple slaw (recipe included). You won't want to make fish tacos any other way. This recipe makes about 8 fish tacos.

Ingredients:
1 Granny Smith apple, cored and julienned
½ red onion, peeled and diced
2 cups Napa cabbage, shredded
¼ cup mayonnaise
¼ cup sour cream
1 teaspoon paprika
salt and pepper to taste
1 ½ pounds Alaska cod
1 tablespoon vegetable oil
1 cup Panko bread crumbs (white or wheat)
1 package of 10 small flour tortilla wrappers

Directions:
1. Make the apple slaw first by putting the apple, onion and cabbage in a large bowl. The cabbage may be very moist, so dab in paper towels before putting it in the bowl.
2. Add the mayonnaise, sour cream, paprika and salt and pepper and make sure everything is coated. Cover and put into the refrigerator until ready to serve.
3. Prepare the fish by cutting it into strips about the size of fast food French fries. These will also be moisture laden so dry them off with paper towels too. Place them in a bowl.
4. Drizzle the vegetable oil over the fish in the bowl.
5. Put the bread crumbs in a closeable plastic bag and add the fish stirps. Only do as many as will fit in the air fryer at a time. If you do not put them directly in the air fryer, they get soggy.
6. Spray the basket of the air fryer with cooking spray and put the fish in a single layer on the bottom of the basket.
7. Cook at 370 degrees F for 12 to 15 minutes or until they are golden and crunchy. Repeat with the rest of the fish.

8. When the fish is almost done, remove the tortillas out of the package and place 5 of them on top of a paper towel in the microwave. Microwave on high20 seconds to get them warm.
9. Place a large tablespoon of the apple slaw in the tortilla and add the fish strips, fold and eat.

Fried Catfish

I do not usually like catfish, but I do like this catfish. It is spicy and wakes up those taste buds and they say "howdy". The texture of the catfish is very crispy and it snaps when you bite into it and then the flavor hits. The breading is cornmeal and flour and that makes it double crunchy. This recipe makes 4 servings and I am now drooling. Time to go find catfish.

Ingredients:
2 pounds catfish fillets
1 cup milk
1 lemon
¼ cup all-purpose flour
½ cup cornmeal
2 tablespoons dried parsley
¼ teaspoon garlic powder
¼ teaspoon onion powder
¼ teaspoon chili powder
¼ teaspoon cayenne pepper
¼ teaspoon Kosher salt
¼ teaspoon black pepper

½ cup yellow mustard
vegetable or olive oil in a mist bottle

Directions:

1. Put the catfish in a deep dish pie plate and cover with milk. Cut the lemon and squeeze 2 teaspoons juice into the milk, you have just made buttermilk. Soak the catfish covered for 15 minutes.
2. When ready to cook, mix the flour, cornmeal, parsley, garlic powder, onion powder, chili powder, cayenne, salt and pepper in another deep dish pie plate and set it aside.
3. Take the fish from the buttermilk and pat it dry with paper towels.
4. Preheat the air fryer to 400 degrees F for 5 minutes.
5. Spread the mustard on both sides of the fillets.
6. Dip into the flour/cornmeal mixture and press so it has a thick coating.
7. Place 2 of the fillets in the nonstick sprayed basket of the air fryer and spray liberally with the oil in the mist bottle.
8. Cook 10 minutes and flip the filets over. Spray with the oil again and cook another 3 to 5 minutes or until brown and crispy.
9. Repeat with other filets.

Fried Fish Cakes

My dad used to make both crab and fish cakes and put them in the freezer. When we forgot to pull something out for dinner, the fish cakes would come out and deep fried. Yes, they did spatter horribly and they were greasy when done. If you use an air fryer, you can still put them in frozen and they will fry up easily without all that greasy flavor and they are actually quite tasty. Serve with tartar sauce and a salad and you have a deliciously quick meal that is light and has few calories. This recipe makes 4 fish cakes and although I use cod, you can also use tuna or salmon. It is also possible to put them in the air fryer right after making them. Just cook them a little less time and watch carefully that they do not burn and turn into hockey pucks. (I did not watch the first time I made them).

Ingredients:
2 large potatoes, peeled and cut in quarters
1 pound cod fillets, cubed
2 tablespoons onion, peeled and chopped very fine
1 tablespoon butter
1 tablespoon fresh parsley, chopped
1 egg
olive oil in a mist bottle

Directions:
1. Place the potatoes in a large pot with water and bring them to a boil. Let them boil until they are nearly tender.
2. Add the fish and boil with the potatoes until both are soft.
3. Drain well and place in a large bowl.
4. Add the onion, butter, parsley and egg and use a potato masher to mash everything together. You can also use a food processor but that sometimes makes the fish cakes less chunky and I like them with chunks of potato and fish.
5. For the mixture into 4 patties and place on a baking sheet. Either freeze or continue to cook in the air fryer.
6. Preheat the air fryer to 360 degrees F for 3 minutes. Place 2 of the patties in the air fryer sprayed with nonstick spray and spray them with olive oil from the mist bottle.
7. Cook 6 minutes, flip, spray again and cook another 5 minutes, if frozen. If not frozen cook 4 minutes, flip and spray and cook another 3 or 4 minutes or until brown and crispy.

Lemon Garlic Shrimp

This shrimp recipe yields 4 servings of some deliciously refreshing citrus flavored shrimp. The flavor is clean and a little spicy because of the garlic and red pepper flakes. It is a delightful dish on a hot summer day.

Ingredients:
1 pound small shrimp, peeled, deveined and tails removed.
1 tablespoon olive oil
4 cloves garlic, peeled and minced
1 pinch crushed red pepper flakes
1 lemon, zested and juiced
¼ teaspoon sea salt
¼ cup fresh parsley, chopped

Directions:
1. Preheat the air fryer to 400 degrees F for 5 minutes.
2. Place the shrimp in a bowl and pour over the olive oil.
3. Add the garlic, red pepper flakes, lemon zest and salt and toss to coat all the shrimp.
4. Spray the basket of the air fryer with nonstick spray and place half the shrimp in the air fryer basket.
5. Cook for 4 minutes, remove the basket and shake vigorously and return to cook another 3 to 4 minutes or until the shrimp

are cooked through. Keep warm until the other half of the shrimp are done.
6. Place shrimp into a serving bowl and toss with the lemon juice and parsley. Add more salt to taste if necessary.

Pesto White Fish Fillets

I give you the recipe to make pesto along with the fish. You can use it with anything. The basil flavor is spectacular with white fish and the outside of the fish is crunchy because of the panko crumbs. If you cannot find pine nuts, or they are too expensive, use almonds instead. This makes 3 servings.

Ingredients:
3 white fillets (about 7 ounces each)
¾ cup plus 1 tablespoon olive oil, divided
salt and pepper to taste
¼ to ½ cup panko bread crumbs
½ cup fresh basil leaves
2 cloves garlic, peeled and minced
2 tablespoons pine nuts

Directions:
1. Preheat the air fryer to 320 degrees F for 3 minutes.
2. Brush the fillets with 1 tablespoon olive oil and season per taste with the salt and pepper.
3. Spray the basket of the air fryer with cooking spray.
4. Place the fillets in the bread crumbs and press in. Place them in the basket of the air fryer.
5. Cook 4 minutes, flip and cook 4 more minutes.
6. While the fish is in the air fryer make the pesto by placing the basil, garlic and pine nuts in a food processor. Process while pouring the ¾ cup olive oil in by drizzling through the chute of the food processor. Process until creamy, taste and add salt and pepper if needed.
7. When the fish is done, place on a serving plate and drizzle them with the pesto. Serve with a side of spaghetti with the pesto.

Ranch Fried Fish Fillets

Use a packet of dry ranch dressing mix to make these fried fish fillets. You can use just about any fish including salmon, but I particularly like using Alaskan cod, sea bass, white fish or even fresh water fish like perch or blue gill. The ranch dressing really gives it some good flavor. Bread the fish and put it immediately into the hot air fryer. This makes 4 servings and I suggest you do the fish in 2 batches, so do not bread the two other fillets until the first two are done.

Ingredients:
1 packet dry ranch dressing mix
¾ cup bread crumbs (I like Panko but you can use regular or crushed cornflakes)
2 ½ tablespoons vegetable oil
¼ cup all-purpose flour
2 eggs, beaten
4 fish fillets
Lemon wedges for garnish and to squeeze on the fish

Directions:
1. Mix the ranch dressing with the bread crumbs and place in a deep dish pie plate. Add the vegetable oil stirring to make a crumbly mixture. I use a fork because it seems to incorporate the oil better. Set the plate aside.
2. Place the flour in a shallow bowl and set aside.
3. Beat the egg in a bowl and set the bowl aside.

4. Preheat the air fryer to 350 degrees F for 5 minutes.
5. Spray the basket with cooking spray.
6. Dip one fillet into the flour mixture and shake excess off.
7. Dip it in the egg next making sure it is completely coated.
8. Dredge in the ranch mixture and press into the fish.
9. Place the fillet into the basket of the air fryer and do the next fillet.
10. Cook for 10 minutes, flip carefully and cook another 2 to 3 minutes depending on thickness of the fillet.
11. Serve with lemon.

Salmon in an Air Fryer

Use salmon fillets that are about 1 to 1 ½ inches thick for this recipe. You will need two for two servings. This recipe is very simple but tasty, but then salmon doesn't need much to make it taste good. Air frying it does not necessarily make it crunchy because you are not breading it. But, if you have ever had trouble cooking salmon, you won't with this recipe. It comes out perfect every time. The recipe says to use olive oil, but I only had avocado oil around and made it with that and it made a world of difference with flavor. I liked it much better. Try it both ways and see what you think.

Ingredients:
2 salmon fillets
2 teaspoons oil (1 for each fillet)

2 teaspoons paprika (1 for each fillet)
Salt and pepper to taste
Lemon wedges for serving

Directions:
1. Remove bones from the fillet if there are any and let the fillet come to room temperature for 1 hour.
2. Preheat your air fryer to 390 degrees for 4 minutes.
3. Rub the fillets with the oil and paprika and then season with salt and pepper.
4. Spray the basket of the air fryer with cooking spray.
5. Depending on how big the fillets are, you may only get one in the air fryer at a time. They should not overlap.
6. Cook for about 4 minutes and flip the fillets. Cook another 3 minutes but keep an eye on them because they may cook faster or slower. You can always pause the air fryer and take a look.
7. Serve with lemon wedges.

Shrimp and Veggies

I use a bag of 50 to 80 small peeled and deveined shrimp for this recipe and a regular sized bag of frozen mixed vegetables. Make sure the shrimp and vegetables are thawed before cooking and that they are well drained. This is one case where you throw everything in the air fryer basket instead of worrying if they are in a single layer. This makes enough for about 4 servings and it is a bit spicy because you are making Cajun seasoning. You probably won't use it all, so bottle it up in an airtight container and keep it for later.

Ingredients:
½ teaspoon onion powder
½ teaspoon garlic powder
½ teaspoon paprika
½ teaspoon Italian seasoning
½ teaspoon sea salt
½ teaspoon black pepper
¼ teaspoon cayenne pepper
½ teaspoon dried thyme
1 bag small shrimp (about 50 to 80 of them) peeled and deveined
1 bag frozen mixed vegetables
olive oil in a spray bottle
Cooked rice for serving

Directions:
1. In a small bowl, combine the onion powder, garlic powder, paprika, Italian seasoning, salt, pepper, cayenne and thyme. Whisk well and set aside.
2. Place all the shrimp and vegetables in the basket of the air fryer after it has been sprayed with nonstick spray.
3. Take 1 tablespoon of the spice mix and sprinkle it on top.
4. Carefully mix with a wooden or rubber spatula to get the spices mixed in.
5. Spray the top with a generous coating of olive oil from a mist bottle.
6. Set the air fryer for 360 degrees and cook for 5 minutes. Open and stir.
7. Cook another 5 minutes and serve over rice.

Traditional Crab Cakes in an Air Fryer

These crab cakes have more crab than filler and they cook up beautifully in an air fryer. You do not even have to flip them half way through the cooking time and I suggest you don't because they tend to break apart. After being fully cooked they stay together. The cakes are crisp on the outside and very moist and delicious so much so, you don't need sauce. A little squeeze of lemon will do the trick. This makes 8 crab cakes.

Ingredients:
2 large eggs
1 tablespoon mayonnaise
1 ¾ teaspoon Old Bay seasoning
1 teaspoon Worcestershire sauce
1 teaspoon Dijon mustard
Salt and pepper to taste
¼ cup green onion, chopped fine
1 pound lump crab meat
½ cup Panko bread crumbs

Directions:
1. Beat the eggs in a bowl and add the mayonnaise, Old Bay, Worcestershire, Dijon, salt and pepper. Mix it well.
2. Add the green onion and fold in.
3. Add the crab and fold in, keeping the crab chunks together and not breaking them apart.
4. Cover with plastic wrap and put in the refrigerator 1 hour.

5. Shape in 8 cakes about 1 inch thick. They should be loosely packed.
6. Preheat the air fryer to 350 degrees F for 4 minutes.
7. Place 4 or less of the crab cakes in the bottom of the basket that has been sprayed with cooking spray.
8. Cook for 5 minutes and flip. Cook for 5 more minutes and serve with lemon wedges.

Tuna Patties Supreme

If you like canned tuna, you will love these patties. They are crispy and moist at the same time and have great flavor using Dijon mustard, lemon juice and parsley. This make 4 patties. Serve with a little tartar sauce, cocktail sauce or nothing at all because they are that good. Make them the night before you are going to cook them. They need to firm up in the refrigerator at least 2 hours so they don't fall apart while cooking.

Ingredients:
2 cans tuna packed in water
½ cup Panko bread crumbs
2 tablespoons fresh parsley, chopped
1 tablespoon lemon juice
1 egg, beaten
2 teaspoons Dijon Mustard
1 dash Tabasco sauce
salt and pepper to taste

Directions:

1. Drain almost all the liquid from the tuna. You want the tuna to feel moist but not watery. Place the tuna in a medium bowl.
2. Add the bread crumbs, parsley, lemon juice, beaten egg, Dijon, Tabasco, salt and pepper.
3. If the mixture seems dry, add a little olive oil and mix it in.
4. Form into 4 patties about 1 inch thick and place on a baking sheet with plastic wrap under and bring it up to cover the patties, otherwise, the refrigerator will smell like tuna for days. Place them in the refrigerator overnight or for at least 2 hours.
5. Preheat the air fryer to 360 for 4 minutes.
6. Place two of the patties in the basket that has been sprayed with cooking spray.
7. Cook 10 minutes and check. If they need more time, cook 2 more minutes but keep checking.
8. Repeat with other two patties.

Beef does well in an air fryer. My favorite beef recipe is coming up next and is Country Fried Steak, but you can also make roast beef. Find out how in the next chapter.

Chapter 7: Beef Meals That Everyone Loves

Not everything comes out crunchy in an air fryer. When you talk about beef, it can come out browned and delicious and super moist. In this chapter you will learn how to make a bunch of beef recipes including beef wellington, roast beef, beef tips, meatloaf, Asian-inspired beef and more. The steak recipe comes out perfect every time I make it and my favorite is the country fried steak with white sausage gravy. Take a look and pick a few recipes to make this week. You won't be sorry.

Beef Fried Rice

Use leftover roast beef or just get some roast beef from the deli counter. Change the recipe up by using pork or chicken and even shrimp. Because you are using rice, it is suggested you use a pan or bowl that fits inside the air fryer basket to make this dish. The rice is little and it flies. It tends to get stuck in the slits of the basket and just makes a mess otherwise. Don't limit yourself to just the vegetables in this recipe. If you have leftover zucchini or summer squash, throw it in or substitute for the peas and carrots. This recipe will serve 4 people.

Ingredients:
3 cups cooked white rice, cold
1 cup frozen peas and carrots, broken up so it can be stirred
½ cup onion, peeled and diced

6 tablespoons light soy sauce
1 tablespoon vegetable oil
1 cup cooked beef, diced (pack it in there)

Directions:
1. Preheat the air fryer to 360 degree F for 4 minutes.
2. Spray a bowl that fits inside the basket with olive oil cooking spray.
3. In a bowl, mix the cold rice, peas and carrots and onions.
4. Add the soy sauce, vegetable sauce and the beef and mix well.
5. Pour into the bowl or pan and cook for 20 minutes, stirring once after 10 minutes.

Beef Jerky In an Air Fryer

This jerky has a little bite to it because of the chili pepper sauce. It is cooked very slow at 180 degrees F (no that is not a misprint) and I use bamboo skewers to hang it over the basket to cook. Be sure to soak those skewers about an hour before cooking so they don't smoke.

Ingredients:
1 pound bottom round beef roast, sliced thin
¼ cup Worcestershire sauce
½ cup soy sauce
1 teaspoon garlic powder
1 teaspoon onion powder
½ teaspoon paprika

½ teaspoon ground black pepper

1 tablespoon liquid smoke

1 tablespoon chili pepper sauce

½ cup dark brown sugar

Directions:

1. Cut the beef in thin strips and set them aside.
2. In a large bowl, mix the Worcestershire sauce, soy sauce, garlic powder, onion powder, paprika and black pepper. Add the liquid smoke, chili pepper sauce and brown sugar and mix well.
3. Place the beef strips in this thick mixture and make sure they are covered. Cover the bowl with plastic wrap and refrigerate overnight.
4. Remove the beef strips and shake off excess sauce. Thread onto the skewers and hang across the basket. I can usually get 5 of them in.
5. Cook at 180 degrees F for 1 hour.
6. Remove from the air fryer and place on a plate with paper towels. Dab any liquid off and let cool.
7. Repeat with other strips.
8. Remove from the skewers and store in an airtight container.

Beef Satay in Peanut Sauce

The peanut sauce in this recipe is deliciously spicy and the meat needs to marinate for 1 hour at least. I like marinating it overnight. Use those bamboo skewers soaked in water about an hour to hold the beef so they do not smoke. This makes enough satay for 4 people for dinner, but it also makes a good appetizer.

Ingredients:
2 tablespoons soy sauce
1 teaspoon garlic, peeled and minced
1 teaspoon fresh ginger, peeled and minced
1 teaspoon sesame oil
½ teaspoon chili garlic sauce
1 ¼ pound New York strip steak, rib eye or fillet, cut in long thin strips

Ingredients for sauce:
2 tablespoons cilantro, chopped
1 tablespoon jalapeno pepper, seeded and chopped
1 tablespoon green onions
½ teaspoon garlic, peeled and minced
¼ teaspoon fresh ginger, peeled and minced
½ cup coconut milk
1/3 cup smooth peanut butter
1 tablespoon fresh lime juice
1 tablespoon hoisin sauce
1 tablespoon fish sauce
Sticky rice for serving over
more cilantro chopped for garnish
Peanuts, roasted and chopped for garnish

Directions:
1. In a bowl, combine the soy sauce, garlic, ginger, sesame oil and chili garlic sauce. Whisk together well.
2. Add the beef strips and toss to coat. Cover and refrigerate at least 1 hour.
3. Thread the beef strips on the skewers and place 4 to 5 of them in the air fryer. Cook at 370 for 10 minutes. Repeat with rest of beef strips.

4. To make the sauce, place the cilantro, jalapeno, green onions, garlic and ginger in a food processor and process on high for about 30 seconds. Place in a bowl, cover and set aside.
5. Put the coconut milk, peanut butter, lime juice, hoisin sauce and fish sauce in the same food processor and blend until smooth and thick.
6. Serve the beef with some sticky rice, chopped cilantro and roasted peanuts.

Beef Tips Air Fryer Style

Serve these beef tips with a salad and some vegetables like broccoli or asparagus. Cooking 8 to 10 minutes produces medium rare beef tips and if you go 10 to 12, you will have something a little more well done. This will serve 4 people.

Ingredients:
1 pound raw top round beef cubes (about 1 inch)
Salt and pepper to taste
1 teaspoon garlic powder
1 teaspoon onion powder
1 tablespoon Worcestershire sauce
1 teaspoon olive oil

Directions:
- Spray the basket of the air fryer with olive oil flavored cooking spray.
- Cut the beef and tenderize the cubes. Season with salt and pepper.
- Combine the garlic powder, onion powder, Worcestershire sauce and olive oil in a bowl and mix well.
- Add the beef and coat all the pieces.
- Spread as many strips as you can get in the bottom of the air fryer without overlapping much.
- Cook at 360 degrees F for 8 to 10 minutes or longer if you like your beef more well done.
-

Country Fried Steak and White Sausage Gravy

This recipe uses sirloin steak that has been pounded to about ¼ inch thick, but I have used round steak or minute steaks that have been tenderized very well. Of course, using sirloin makes the tastiest country fried steak but sometimes that can be pretty expensive. The main thing is to tenderize it well and pound it thin. The meat comes out crispy on the outside and juicy inside and I have included the gravy because what is country fried steak without that white sausage gravy. This makes 4 servings.

Ingredients:
1 cup Panko bread crumbs
1 teaspoon garlic powder
1 teaspoon onion powder
1 teaspoon salt
½ teaspoon pepper
1 cup flour
3 eggs beaten
4 6-ounce sirloin steaks, pounded thin

Directions:
1. Mix the panko, garlic powder, onion powder, salt and pepper in a shallow bowl and set it aside.
2. Place the flour in another shallow bowl and set it aside.
3. Beat the eggs in yet another bowl and set them aside.
4. Pound the steaks and preheat the air fryer to 370 degrees for 5 minutes.

5. Dredge the steaks, one at a time, in the flour and shake off excess.
6. Dip in the egg and coat them well.
7. Dredge in the panko making sure to press the crumbs in so they stick well.
8. Spray the basket of the air fryer and place 1 or 2 of the steaks in it.
9. Cook at 370 degrees F for 6 minutes, turn and cook another 6 minutes.
10. To make the sausage gravy cook the sausage until it is done and retain 2 tablespoons of the fat in the pan.
11. Add the flour and mix well.
12. Slowly add the milk stirring constantly and heat until it thickens.
13. Add the pepper and stir in.
14. Serve over the meat.

Easy Beef Stir Fry

This recipe is delicious and the vegetables retain their integrity and do not get mushy. The sauce is particularly tasty and you can actually substitute other vegetables like green beans, peas, cauliflower or anything else. It makes 4 servings.

Ingredients:
2 tablespoons garlic, peeled and minced
1 tablespoon soy sauce

1 teaspoon sesame oil
1 teaspoon fresh ginger, peeled and grated
¼ cup water
1 pound beef sirloin, cut in 2 strips
1 red pepper, cut into strips
1 green pepper, cut into strips
1 yellow pepper, cut into strips
1 ½ pounds broccoli florets
1 cup onion, peeled and diced
Olive oil in a mist bottle
Cooked rice for serving

Directions:

1. In a bowl combine the garlic, soy sauce, sesame oil, ginger and water. Whisk well, cover and place in the refrigerator for 20 minutes.
2. Spray the basket of the air fryer place the peppers, broccoli and onion in the basket. Spray generously with the olive oil and cook at 200 degrees F for 5 minutes. The vegetables should be soft but not mushy. Pour into a bowl and set aside.
3. Place the meat strips in the air fryer and increase the temperature to 360 degrees F and cook for 4 minutes, turn and cook another 2 minutes.
4. Place the cooked rice on a plate, top with the vegetables and then add the meat.

Herbed Roast Beef and Potatoes

This roast is reminiscent of the one my grandmother used to make with the flavor of rosemary and thyme. It has a lovely flavor and you make red potatoes to go with it. It makes 4 generous servings. Most air fryer recipes want you to place everything in one layer in the basket but this one is different. You just pile the potatoes right on top of the roast and let them cook.

Ingredients:

2 teaspoons olive oil
1 4-pound top round roast
1 teaspoon garlic powder
½ teaspoon fresh rosemary, chopped
1 teaspoon dried thyme
1 teaspoon salt
½ teaspoon ground black pepper
3 pounds red potatoes, cut in fourths
olive oil
salt and pepper to taste

Directions:

- Preheat the air fryer to 360 degrees F for 5 minutes.
- Rub the olive oil on all sides of the roast.
- Combine the garlic powder, rosemary, thyme, salt and pepper in a small bowl and apply it to the roast liberally on all sides.

- Spray the inside basket of the air fryer with cooking spray and place the roast in.
- Cook for 20 minutes.
- While cooking cut the potatoes and place them in a bowl with enough olive oil to coat them well.
- Remove the basket from the air fryer and flip the roast over. Pour in the red potatoes and let them go down the sides of the roast.
- Cook for another 20 minutes. Check internal temperature for rare at 130, medium at 140 or well done at 160. Cook a little longer or take the roast out and let it rest.
- Do not take the potatoes out. Cook the potatoes an extra 8 to 10 minutes removing and shaking the basket every 3 minutes until they are done.
- Let the roast rest at least 6 minutes before carving. Serve with the potatoes and a vegetable on the side.

Elegant Beef Wellington

I always think Beef Wellington along with Chef Gordon Ramsey screaming at his chefs for not doing it right. With this recipe there would be no yelling because it comes out perfect every time. Most wellingtons are coated with a liver pate, and I hate liver pate. This one is coated with a mushroom pate that is much more palatable and delicious.   Use refrigerated pie crust that comes in package and rolls out flat. This makes 4 to 6 servings.

Ingredients:

1 4-pound beef fillet
salt and pepper to taste
1 cup mushrooms, chopped (I use baby bella mushrooms)
¼ teaspoon dried thyme
¼ teaspoon dried rosemary
½ to 1 teaspoon olive oil
1 refrigerated pie crust
1 egg beaten

Directions:

1. Remove any extra fat from the beef fillet and season with salt and pepper. Cover with plastic wrap and place in the refrigerator at least 1 hour or overnight.
2. Place the mushrooms, thyme and rosemary in the bowl of a food processor and process while pouring in the olive oil through the chute. This should be like a thick paste that is spreadable. Add a little more olive oil to thin it or more mushrooms to thicken it.
3. Place the pie dough on a flat surface and roll out.
4. Take a pastry bush and brush all the edges with the egg.
5. Spread the mushroom pate to 1 ½ inch of the edge of the pie crust.
6. Preheat the air fryer to 320 degrees F for 4 minutes. When done, spray the basket with cooking spray.
7. Unwrap the fillet and place it on top of the pie crust a little down from the middle.
8. Fold the pie crust over top and seal the edges. The olive oil should help it stick.
9. Score the top so that steam can escape and place the Wellington in the basket of the air fryer. Brush more egg in a thin layer over the top of the Wellington.
10. Cook 35 minutes. Check for internal temperature for about 140 degrees for medium rare before removing. The crust should be brown but not burned.
11. Remove and let sit for about 8 minutes before cutting and serving.

Garlic Butter Air Fryer Steak

Butter on steak, especially with garlic, is a delicious combination and this one is no different. The rib eye is enhanced with butter infused with garlic. The recipe makes a log of butter that you can use on other things as well. There is plenty left over. The recipe serves 2 people.

Ingredients:
1 stick unsalted butter, room temperature
1 teaspoon Worcestershire sauce
2 teaspoons garlic, peeled and minced
2 tablespoons fresh parsley, chopped
¼ teaspoon salt
2 8-ounce Ribeye steaks
olive oil
salt and pepper to taste

Directions:
1. Make the garlic butter about 1 to 2 hours before cooking or overnight. Place the softened butter in a bowl and mix with the Worcestershire, garlic, parsley and salt. Mix it in completely.

2. Scoop the butter onto a piece of parchment paper and roll it into a log. Secure the ends and place in the refrigerator 2 hours or overnight. You want it to become stiff.
3. When ready to cook the steak, rub the steaks on both sides with olive oil and salt and pepper to taste.
4. Rub more olive oil on the basket bottom and sides of the air fryer and preheat at 400 degrees F for 4 minutes.
5. Place the steaks in the basket, if they won't both fit without overlapping each other, do them separately and watch because the time to cook will be shorter.
6. Cook 5 to 6 minutes, flip and cook another 5 to 6 minutes. Let the steaks rest a few minutes and cut off a piece of the cold butter and place it on top. Make it a generous piece. The butter will melt over the steak.
7. Serve immediately.

Hot Mongolian Beef

This is a dish you might find in a Chinese restaurant and it is made with flank steak. Flank steak is a little flatter than other types of steak and it is denser. It cuts into strips easily but if you leave it slightly frozen when you cut it, you will be able to cut the slices very thin. This recipe makes 4 servings. Serve the beef over hot cooked rice and sprinkle some chopped green onions over top.

Ingredients:

1 1-pound flank steak
¼ cup cornstarch
2 teaspoons vegetable oil
1 tablespoon garlic, peeled and minced
½ teaspoon fresh ginger, peeled and grated
½ cup water
½ cup soy sauce
¾ cup brown sugar, packed
Cooked Rice
Sliced green onions

Directions:
1. Slice the flank steak in long thin strips and place in a bowl. Sprinkle the cornstarch over it and toss so the meat is coated.
2. Spray the basket of the air fryer with cooking spray and set for 390 cooking the meat for 10 minutes on each side.
3. While the meat cooks, whisk the vegetable oil, garlic, ginger, water, soy sauce and brown sugar in a sauce pan over medium heat. When it starts to boil slowly, turn it down so it just simmers until the beef is done.
4. Place the steak in the pan with the hot sauce and let it soak about 5 minutes covering the pot.
5. Place rice on a plate or in a bowl and take the beef strips out with tongs, shake off excess liquid and place on top of the rice. Pour a little sauce over top and sprinkle with green onions.

Meatloaf in an Air Fryer

This meatloaf comes out browned and beautiful with little mushrooms embedded in the top. Once you make meatloaf in an air fryer you will not want to make it in the oven again. You know how that grease collects at the bottom of the pan and the meatloaf ends up swimming in it. That doesn't happen as much in an air fryer. If you want a little kick spread some ketchup or thick tomato sauce on top of the meatloaf before cooking. This recipe serves 4 people.

Ingredients:
1 egg, lightly beaten
1 small onion, peeled and finely chopped
1 ½ teaspoons garlic, peeled and minced
½ tablespoon fresh thyme chopped
¼ teaspoon Italian Seasoning
1 pinch crushed red pepper flakes
1 teaspoon salt
½ teaspoon pepper
¼ cup dry bread crumbs
3 tablespoons water or ketchup
1 pound lean ground beef
2 large mushrooms, sliced thick
1 tablespoon or more olive oil

Directions:
1. Beat the egg in a large bowl and add the onion, garlic, thyme, Italian seasoning, red pepper flakes, salt and pepper. Mix with a fork.
2. Add the water or ketchup and mix in.
3. Preheat the air fryer to 390 degrees for 4 minutes.
4. Add the bread crumbs and mix in well.
5. Add the ground beef and use hands to mix everything in well. Form into a loaf and place in a pan that fits inside the air fryer basket that has been treated with cooking spray.
6. Place the sliced mushrooms on top of the meatloaf and press in. Brush liberally with the olive oil.

7. Cook 25 minutes and test internal temperature. It should read about 160 degrees F.
8. Remove the meatloaf from the basket and place on a cutting board. Let rest 6 to 10 minutes and cut in slices.

Mexican Carne Asada

Carne Asada is a caramelized beef dish where the meat is grilled and charred with spices and citrus juices mixed in. You can get about the same flavor in your air fryer. Serve the meat with tortilla wraps and fill with lettuce, cabbage, tomatoes, onions and salsa for a great meal. Sprinkle with some fresh cilantro and fresh squeezed lime juice.

Ingredients:
2 Padilla peppers
4 whole Chipotle peppers in Adobo (they are in a can)
¼ cup fresh squeezed lime juice
¼ cup fresh squeezed lemon juice
½ cup fresh squeezed orange juice
6 cloves garlic, peeled and minced
2 tablespoons olive oil
1 cup fresh cilantro
1 teaspoon Kosher salt
½ teaspoon ground black pepper
2 tablespoons light brown sugar
2 teaspoons dried oregano

1 teaspoon ground cumin

2 pounds skirt steak, cut ½-inch thick or a little more

1 large onion, peeled and thinly sliced

Directions:

1. In a food processor, place the Padilla peppers, chipotle peppers, lime juice, lemon juice, orange juice, garlic, olive oil, cilantro, salt, pepper, brown sugar, oregano and cumin and process for 20 seconds. This will create a thick sauce.
2. Remove ½ cup to use as a salsa when serving.
3. Pour the rest of the sauce into a large plastic closeable bag and add the steak and onion. Close and marinate 3 hours or overnight.
4. When ready to cook, preheat the air fryer to 400 degrees F for 10 minutes. Spray with cooking spray.
5. Remove the steak and onions from the bag. I use tongs. Put them in the prepared basket of the air fryer and cook at 400 degrees F for 10 to 12 minutes. This will give you medium rare steak. Let it go a little longer if you want it more well done.
6. Remove the steak and onions from the air fryer and let rest 5 minutes. Slice the skirt steak on an angle as thin as possible and serve in tortilla wrappers with a little of the reserved sauce and other fresh vegetables.

Moroccan Meatballs With Mint Yogurt Dip!

These meatballs are delicious with their mint flavor in the meatballs and in the dip that goes with them. The spices give them an exotic flavor with coriander and cumin. I use paprika instead of cayenne because I don't like food to be too spicy. The red chili paste is optional if you like hot food, I don't use it because your tongue is so affected with the spice, it seems hard to taste the delicious minty dip. This recipe makes 16 meatballs and I like to serve them with some rice.

Ingredients for Meatballs:
1 teaspoon ground coriander
1 teaspoon ground cumin
1 teaspoon cayenne pepper or paprika
1 teaspoon red chili paste (optional)
2 large cloves of garlic, peeled and minced
¼ cup bread crumbs
1 tablespoon fresh mint, chopped fine
2 tablespoons fresh flat leaf parsley, chopped fine
salt and pepper to taste
1 egg
1 pound lean ground beef

Ingredients for Mint Yogurt Dip:
¼ cup sour cream
½ cup plain Greek yogurt
2 tablespoons buttermilk
1 small clove garlic, peeled and chopped fine
2 heaping tablespoons fresh mint, chopped fine
2 tablespoons honey
salt and pepper to taste

Directions:
1. In a large bowl, whisk together the coriander, cumin and cayenne or paprika.
2. Add the chili paste, garlic, bread crumbs, mint, parsley and salt and pepper and mix well.
3. Add the beaten egg and incorporate into the mixture.
4. Add the beef and use the hands to mix everything in.

5. Spray the basket of the air fryer with cooking spray and form 2-inch diameter balls with the mixture. Place 8 in the air fryer at a time (that is half of the meatballs).
6. Brush or spray the meatballs with a little oil.
7. Cook at 390 degrees F for 8 minutes. Remove with tongs to a bowl.
8. Repeat with the other 8 meatballs.
9. While cooking the meatballs make the dip by placing the sour cream, yogurt, buttermilk, garlic, mint and honey. Mix and taste. You may decide you need salt and pepper or you may not, it is up to you.
10. Dip the meatballs in the yogurt dip when eating them.

Parmesan Meat Balls

Here is another meatball recipe and these have Parmesan cheese in them. You can use them in a meatball sandwich or with pasta and sauce. Marinara sauce is cooked right in the meatballs and that makes them very moist with a lovely brown coat on the outside from air frying. This recipe makes 12 meatballs.

Ingredients:
1 and ½ cup Marinara sauce, divided
1 tablespoon dried minced onions
1 teaspoon Italian seasoning
1 teaspoon garlic powder

169

1/3 cup Parmesan, shredded or grated (fresh)
½ teaspoon salt
¼ teaspoon pepper
1 egg
1 pound lean ground beef
Shredded Mozzarella Cheese

Directions:

1. Place ¼ cup of the marinara sauce in a bowl and add the onions, Italian seasoning, garlic powder and Parmesan. Mix well.
2. Add the egg and mix it in.
3. Add the ground beef and use your hands to incorporate everything into the beef.
4. Form into 12 meatballs and place them in the cooking sprayed basket of the air fryer. If they do not all fit, cook in two batches.
5. Set the air fryer for 350 degrees F and cook for 11 minutes.
6. While the meatballs are cooking, heat up the rest of the marinara in a saucepan on the stove.
7. Open the air fryer and sprinkle a little mozzarella cheese on top of the meat balls. Cook at 350 degrees F for 2 to 3 more minutes.
8. Use tongs to remove the meatballs and place them in a bowl. Pour the heated marinara over top and sprinkle with more mozzarella to serve.

Reuben Egg Rolls:

This is an odd sort of recipe using egg roll wrappers instead of rye bread to make a corned beef Rueben. I use corned beef you get in the deli, sliced thin and it works very well. You may think it sounds strange, but this recipe is super good. There are no increments added to the ingredients. Use your judgement to fill the egg roll wrappers and not get too much in them. Make as many as you like, but make sure to eat them right away because they don't keep well. I made four of them for dinner for two people but it also depends on how big the egg roll wrappers are. When I make them for a crowd, I can get four eggrolls in the air fryer basket. I also make some without sauerkraut and serve with a bowl of coleslaw. I dip my Rueben egg roll in the coleslaw and take a bite.

Ingredients:
Egg Roll Wrappers
Deli Corned Beef
1 small can Sauerkraut, drained, rinsed and dry pressed with paper towels
Swiss cheese
Cooking Spray (I do not like olive oil, because of the flavor with sauerkraut. Use butter or vegetable oil spray)
1000 Island Dressing and/or Coleslaw

Directions:
1. Lay an eggroll wrapper on a flat surface and moisten the edges with a little water so it sticks when you fold and seal it.
2. Place it with the point of a corner toward the middle of your body.
3. Place a piece of Swiss on top of the egg roll wrapper and then a piece of corned beef. Place another piece of cheese, corned beef and Swiss. If your corned beef is thin, use two slices instead of one for a layer.
4. Spread a little sauerkraut on top.
5. Take the pointed end toward you and fold it all the way over the contents. Bring up the sides and fold in. Fold over again until you get something that looks like an egg roll.
6. Place them in the air fryer basket leaving a little room between each. Spray with cooking spray lightly.
7. Cook at 400 degrees F for 4 minutes. Flip them over and cook another 4 minutes.
8. Serve with a dip of 1000 Island Dressing and/or coleslaw.

Roast Beef in an Air Fryer

Air fryers are known to make things crispy and the outside of the beef roast does get delightfully crispy, but the inside is near perfect if you like medium to medium rare roasts. It is also great if you like it a little more well done. Always test for doneness with an internal thermometer. Rare should be around 130 degrees F, Medium 140 degrees F, Medium well at 150 degrees F and Well done at 160 degrees. If you think the temperature is too low for you, put the roast in for another 4 minutes and test again. Always let the roast rest at least 8 minutes so the juices don't come pouring out when you cut it in slices. This gives them time to permeate the roast. I think an eye of round roast is the best for this recipe, but you can use other types of beef roast as well. A 2-pound roast will feed 6 people.

Ingredients:
1 tablespoon olive oil
1 teaspoon dried rosemary
½ teaspoon garlic powder
1 teaspoon sea salt
½ teaspoon pepper
1 2-pound beef roast

Directions:

1. Preheat the air fryer to 360 degrees F for 8 minutes.
2. Place the oil on a plate and mix in the rosemary, garlic powder, salt and pepper. Spread out the mixture on the plate.
3. Set the beef roast top side down, on the plate and press down so that the oil soaks into the top. Also rub the roast on the bottom and sides in the oil mixture.
4. Spray the basket of the air fryer with cooking spray and set the roast in. Cook for 45 minutes and test the internal temperature. Put in 4 to 8 more minutes depending on the degree of doneness desired.

Sizzling Steak Fajitas

These fajitas do sizzle as they come out of the air fryer and they are simply delicious. Serve on warmed corn tortillas sprinkled with a little Mexican cheese and you have a great meal fit for a king. Serve sour cream and guacamole on the side. This recipe will feed 4 people.

Ingredients:

¼ teaspoon garlic powder
¼ teaspoon chili powder
¼ teaspoon dried oregano

½ teaspoon ground cumin
1 teaspoon salt
½ teaspoon ground pepper
2 tablespoons olive oil
2 medium bell peppers (I use green and red), seeded and sliced in strips
2 serrano peppers, chopped
½ red onion, peeled and sliced thin
½ yellow onion, peeled and sliced thin
1 pound beef, sliced into thin strips
Shredded Mexican cheese (you can use Cheddar)
Corn Tortillas

Directions:

1. Combine the garlic powder, chili powder, oregano, cumin, salt and pepper with the olive oil and mix well.
2. Place the peppers, onions and beef in the bowl and toss to coat all the vegetables and the meat.
3. Spray a pan that fits into the air fryer with nonstick spray and pour the vegetables and meat in.
4. Cook at 390 degrees F and cook for 6 minutes. Open and stir the meat and vegetables around. Cook another 4 to 5 minutes and serve with cheese sprinkled over top in a corn tortilla.

Spicy Coffee Rubbed Steak

If you have never had a coffee and spice rubbed piece of beef, you are missing out on something. The coffee gives the beef an exotic and rich flavor and you will be very impressed with this entrée. This makes one steak that can be separated into two servings and I use ribeye steaks just because they fit better in the air fryer basket. The secret ingredient to this recipe is the cocoa powder. It combines with the brown sugar and coffee and makes spectacular flavor.

Ingredients:

1 teaspoon Kosher salt
½ teaspoon ground black pepper
1 teaspoon brown sugar
½ teaspoon ground coffee
¼ teaspoon chipotle powder
¼ teaspoon chili powder
¼ teaspoon onion powder
¼ teaspoon garlic powder
¼ teaspoon paprika
1/8 teaspoon coriander
1/8 teaspoon cocoa powder
1 1-pound ribeye steak

Directions:

1. In a small bowl, whisk together the salt, pepper, brown sugar, coffee, chipotle powder, chili powder, onion powder, garlic powder, paprika, coriander and cocoa powder. Make sure the brown sugar breaks up and you have a smooth mixture.
2. Sprinkle a generous amount of this spice mixture on a dinner plate and spread it out.
3. Place the steak on top and press it down so it transfers to the steak. Flip and do the same on the other side. Press so that all the spice mixture is on the steak.
4. Preheat the air fryer to 390 degrees F for 4 minutes. Spray the basket with cooking spray and place the steak in.
5. Cook for 9 minutes, do not flip or open the air fryer.
6. Remove with tongs to sit on a plate 5 minutes before slicing and serving.

Spinach and Cheese Steak Roll

When you pick your steak to make this dish remember that you must pound it to ¼-inch thin and roll everything in it. Avoid thick steaks. You will need butcher string to tie up the roll and it stays on while it cooks. Snip it off when done cooking and the roll should stay rolled. This is an elegant meal to serve for your family or for a special guest.

Ingredients:
2 larger sized sirloin steaks
salt, pepper and garlic powder to taste
1 bag baby spinach, you will not use it all so use it in a salad to serve along side
5 slices Provolone

Directions:
1. Pound the steaks to 1/4- inch thin and cut 4 to 5 pieces out of the 2 steaks.
2. Season both sides of each piece with the salt, pepper and garlic powder.
3. Lay a piece of cheese on top of each piece, cutting it to fit if necessary and also a handful of baby spinach.
4. Roll like a jelly roll and tie with the butcher string to keep them closed.
5. Spray the inside basket of the air fryer with cooking spray and place the rolls in.
6. Cook 400 degrees for 8 minutes, use tongs to turn the rolls and cook another 6 minutes.
7. Remove from the air fryer basket and let rest 10 minutes before cutting into medallions and serving.

Stuffed Peppers

The first time I made these the peppers came out pretty charred and you couldn't eat them. That taught me to watch the timing carefully because even though a recipe says to cook something 10 minutes, it doesn't mean it is going to work in your air fryer. I cut the lumps off the bottoms of my peppers so they sit upright without falling over. It makes for a flat surface on the bottom of the pepper. I chop these up with the tops I cut off, discarding the stem, and use them in the mixture. This makes 2 stuffed peppers and I had a little meat left over, but I probably could have stuffed the peppers a little more. Try this recipe with bulk ground Italian sausage instead of the ground beef.

Ingredients:
2 medium green peppers, stems, tops and seeds removed and rinsed.
1 clove garlic, peeled minced
½ medium onion, peeled and chopped
1 teaspoon olive oil
8 ounces lean ground beef
¼ cup minute rice
1 teaspoon Worcestershire sauce
½ cup tomato sauce, divided
½ teaspoon salt
¼ teaspoon black pepper
4 ounces Mozzarella cheese

Directions:

1. Bring a pot of water to boil on the stove and place the prepared green peppers in. Boil ONLY 3 minutes and pour into a colander. Rinse with cold water to stop them from cooking. The peppers should not be soft. Turn them upside down to drain while making the filling.
2. Sauté the garlic and onion in the olive oil in a skillet on the stove and cool.
3. Place the beef in a large bowl and add the minute rice, Worcestershire sauce, ¼ cup of the tomato sauce, salt and pepper. Mix well with hands and add the cooled garlic and onions mixing it in well with half of the shredded cheese.
4. Stuff each pepper with half the mixture.
5. Preheat the air fryer to 380 degrees F for 4 minutes.
6. Spray the basket with cooking spray and place the peppers in. Cook for 15 minutes. The internal temperature should be close to 160 degrees F. If not put them in a few more minutes.
7. Pour the rest of the sauce over each pepper and top with the rest of the cheese. Cook another 3 to 5 minutes but watch so the peppers and cheese do not turn black and burn.

Now that we have a bunch of beef recipes we can now proceed to the Pork chapter and learn how to make luscious pork chops, pork roasts, ham and more.

Chapter 8: Pork and Ham Recipes That Will Thrill Your Taste Buds

I love down home country cooking and some of the best meals I have ever had in that category are ones made from pork. Pork roasts, pork chops, pork ribs and pork chops can be some of the easiest dinners to make, but they can turn around and be very elegant as well. I know we have glazed ham every Christmas holiday and you can glaze a ham and cook it in an air fryer. Pork Roasts and chops come out succulently juicy and crisp on the outside and although ribs are hard to get in the air fryer, it is so worth it when you are done. Try a few of the following recipes and see if they do not become a family favorite.

Asian Style Salt and Pepper Chops

You will find Salt and Pepper chops in good Chinese restaurants. The chop does not require a bone, so I get boneless pork chops and cut them into small pieces. The meat is very crunchy and brown and instead of using expensive and really, really hot Asian peppers, I have used jalapenos. This recipe makes 2 servings.

Ingredients:
1 egg white
½ teaspoon sea salt
¼ teaspoon ground black pepper

2 to 3 boneless pork chops

¾ cup potato starch (can use cornstarch)

Oil in an oil mist bottle (I used peanut)

2 tablespoons peanut oil

2 green onions, trimmed and sliced

2 jalapeno peppers, stems removed, seeded and sliced

1 teaspoon sea salt

¼ teaspoon ground black pepper

Directions:

1. Whisk the egg white, salt and pepper in a bowl until it is foamy.
2. Cut the pork chops in pieces and place in the bowl making sure to coat each piece well.
3. Cover and refrigerate 20 minutes.
4. Remove the chop pieces from the egg white bowl and drop into the potato starch. Coat evenly.
5. Preheat the air fryer to 390 degrees F.
6. Spray the air fryer basket with the oil in the mist bottle and place the chop pieces in the basket. Spray them liberally with the oil as well.
7. Cook for 9 minutes shaking the basket frequently. Turn the chop pieces, spray with oil and put in for another 4 to 6 minutes or until brown and crispy.
8. Heat up a wok on the stove and spray some oil into it. Sauté the onions, jalapenos, salt and pepper for about 1 minute.
9. Add the pork and sauté 2 to 3 minutes.
10. Serve with rice.

Bacon Wrapped Pork Tenderloin

This roast has the flavors of bacon, because of wrapping, but also has the taste of onions and apples. This makes a great family dinner and also is nicely elegant meal for guests. The roast serves 4 to 6 people and goes nicely with air fried Brussel sprouts and other vegetables.

Ingredients:
1 to 2 tablespoons Dijon mustard
1 pork tenderloin
3 to 4 strips bacon
2 tablespoons butter, divided
1 small onion, peeled and chopped
2 to 3 Granny Smith apples, peeled, cored and cut in slices
1 tablespoon flour
1 cup vegetable broth
salt and pepper to taste
Garnish with fresh chopped rosemary, parsley and thyme

Directions:
1. Preheat the air fryer to 360 for about 5 minutes.
2. Spread the mustard onto the pork loin and wrap it with uncooked bacon.
3. Place it in the air fryer basket that has been treated with cooking spray and cook 15 minutes.

4. Turn the roast and cook another 10 to 15 minutes until brown and crisp on the outside. Check that internal temperature is around 145 degrees F.
5. Heat 1 teaspoon of the butter in a saucepan and sauté the onions 1 to 2 minutes.
6. Add the apple slices and sauté 3 to 5 minutes or until soft. Pour the onions and apples into a bowl and set it aside.
7. Use the same pan and add the remaining butter, melting it.
8. Stir in the flour to make a roux.
9. Slowly add the broth while stirring until it is well combined and not lumpy. Let it come to a simmer with bubbles forming around the edges. It will thicken. Add the apple and onion mixture and stir in well.
10. Slice the roast after it rests about 5 to 8 minutes and pour the gravy over top.

Barbeque Pork Ribs – Finger Lickin' Good

You will want to like the plate, not only your fingers when you have these ribs for dinner. The hardest part is fitting the ribs into the air fryer. You get two racks and set them on end leaning them against the side of the air fryer basket and crisscrossing each other. Once you make BBQ ribs with this rub, you will want no other kind. It makes 2 servings.

Ingredients:
1 tablespoon dark brown sugar

1 teaspoon onion powder

1 teaspoon garlic powder

1 tablespoon paprika (sweet)

1 teaspoon poultry seasoning

½ teaspoon prepared mustard powder

1 tablespoon kosher salt

½ teaspoon ground black pepper

2 ¼-pounds St Louis-style pork spareribs

Directions:

1. In a bowl, whisk the brown sugar, onion powder, garlic powder, paprika, poultry seasoning, mustard powder, salt and pepper.
2. Rub this mixture into the ribs on both sides until it is completely covered.
3. Spray the basket of the air fryer with cooking spray and place the ribs in on end leaning against the basket crossing each other.
4. Set the temperature to 350 degrees F and cook 35 minutes.
5. The ribs come out brown and crispy.

Beer Glazed Ham Steak

I use light beer or near beer to make this recipe. The glaze is delicious and I serve with mashed or boiled potatoes with some of the glaze poured on them too. The alcohol does cook out before you eat it. Use ham steaks and contain them and the glaze. You do need a pan that fits inside the air fryer to make this dish. If the ham steaks are too big, just cut them to fit. This makes 3 servings.

Ingredients:

3 8-ounce ham steaks

2 12-ounce cans beer

1 cup brown sugar

1 tablespoon Dijon mustard

2 tablespoons balsamic vinegar

Directions:

1. Place the ham steaks in a baking dish and pour 1 can of beer over top. Cover with plastic wrap and put in the refrigerator 3 hours to marinate.
2. When ready to make, start with the glaze.
3. In another pan mix the brown sugar, Dijon and balsamic vinegar.
4. Add 1/3 of the other can of beer and whisk well.
5. Place 1 ham steak in the pan that fits into the air fryer and pour some glaze over top.
6. Place another ham steak on top and cover with glaze. Top with another steak and more glaze.
7. Air fry at 380 degrees F for 10 to 15 minutes or until brown and gooey.
8. Heat up any leftover glaze and serve it alongside.

Brown Sugar Ham Steak

This recipe makes one 8-ounce ham steak, so if you need two, you need to make it in 2 batches. The good thing is that you can get the ham steaks already at the same time and because everything is wrapped in foil, placed in the air fryer and cooked inside the foil and because the ham is already cooked, it doesn't take long (about 8 minutes) for the ham steak to cook. Just keep the previously cooked one folded up in its foil until all are done.

Ingredients:
1 8-ounce bone in fully cooked ham steak
5 tablespoons butter, in slices
5 tablespoons brown sugar

Directions:
1. Lay a piece of foil big enough to completely fold the ham steak in on a flat surface and place the steak in the middle.
2. Melt the butter (I do it in the microwave) and add the brown sugar. Stir until combined.
3. Spread half the thick butter/brown sugar spread on the ham steak and turn it over.
4. Spread the rest on the side of the ham steak.
5. Pre heat the air fryer to 380 degrees F for 4 minutes.

6. Fold the foil up and over the ham steak creating an envelope that will not leak over the steak.
7. Place the folded ham steak in the basket of the air fryer and cook for 8 minutes.
8. Remove from the air fryer and carefully unfold the foil watching for steam. The ham steak should be done and coated with the rich brown sugar and butter sauce.
9. If you are making more than one ham steak, be careful. It might not take as long to cook subsequent steaks because the air fryer will be hot.

Crispy Boneless Pork Chops

This recipe is a basic breaded pork chop recipe that everyone will like. Instead of deep fryer or cooking in oil or butter in the stove, it is cooked in the air fryer and that reduces the amount of grease that come with pork chops. I use center cut boneless chops about ¾ inch thick and do three at a time in 2 batches. I place one on the bottom and the others I lay up against the sides of the air fryer. They do touch, but most of the surface of the chops are exposed. This recipe makes 4 deliciously crispy pork chops.

Ingredients:
6 pork chops with fat trimmed
1 teaspoon kosher salt, divided
1/3 cup crushed cornflake crumbs
½ cup panko bread crumbs
½ teaspoon garlic powder

½ teaspoon onion powder

1 ¼ teaspoon paprika

¼ teaspoon chili powder

2 tablespoons grated Parmesan cheese

1/8 teaspoon black pepper

1 egg, beaten

Olive oil in a mist bottle

Directions:

1. Season the chops on both sides with ½ teaspoon of the salt and set them aside.
2. In a shallow bowl, combine the cornflakes, panko crumbs, garlic powder, onion powder, paprika, chili powder, Parmesan cheese, pepper and the remaining salt.
3. Mix well and set the bowl aside.
4. Whisk the egg in another bowl and set it aside.
5. Preheat the air fryer to 400 degrees F for 8 minutes
6. Dip the chops in the egg and then in the crumb mixture pressing it in on both sides.
7. Place three of the chops in and spray liberally with oil.
8. Cook for 6 minutes, turn and spray with oil again and cook another 6 minutes.
9. Repeat with other chops.

Easy Pork Loin Roast with Red Potatoes

This recipe is super easy. Just season the roast, put it in the air fryer, cut the potatoes and put them around the roast and cook. That is pretty much all there is to it. The recipe makes enough for 4 people and it might take the potatoes a little longer to cook than the roast, but that is fine since you must wait about 8 minutes to cut the roast after it is done.

Ingredients:
1 2-pound pork loin
olive oil in a mist bottle
4 to 5 red potatoes, skin on, diced large
½ teaspoon garlic powder
½ teaspoon red pepper flakes
1 teaspoon dried parsley
½ teaspoon kosher salt
½ teaspoon black pepper

Directions:
1. Trim any excess fat from the pork loin and spray it liberally with olive oil. Set the roast aside.
2. Dice the potatoes and set them aside.
3. In a small bowl combine the garlic powder, red pepper flakes, parsley, salt and pepper and spread a little more than half on the top and sides of the pork loin. Set the loin in the basket of the air fryer that has been sprayed with olive oil.
4. Toss the potatoes with the remaining garlic powder mixture and pour into the basket down the sides and on top of the roast. Keep the potatoes to the side so the very top of the roast browns.
5. Spray the potatoes and roast with more olive oil.
6. Cook at 390 degrees F for 35 minutes. Test with a meat thermometer to make sure the roast reaches 145 degrees F internal temperature. If not put it back in for a few more minutes.
7. Once it is done, remove the roast and test the potatoes. If they are still hard, spread them out in the basket, spray with more olive oil and cook 4 to 5 minutes until they are soft.

8. Slice the loin after resting 8 minutes and serve with the potatoes.

Garlic Butter Pork Chops

These luscious chops are made with coconut butter, coconut oil and garlic and taste divine providing you like garlic. Wrap them in aluminum foil, put them in the refrigerator overnight or at least 2 hours and place them, two at a time in the air fryer to cook. This makes 4 pork chops.

Ingredients:
2 teaspoons parsley
¼ teaspoon pepper
½ teaspoon kosher salt
2 teaspoons grated garlic
1 tablespoon coconut oil
1 tablespoon coconut butter
4 pork chops

Directions:
1. Mix the parsley, salt, pepper, garlic, coconut oil and coconut butter and mix with a rubber spatula squishing everything together so it is well mixed.
2. Take your hands and rub the mixture in all pork chops on both sides.

3. Fold into aluminum foil and refrigerate at least 2 hours or overnight.
4. When ready to cook, preheat the air fryer to 350 degrees F for 5 minutes.
5. Unwrap the chops from the aluminum and place 2 of them in a pan that fits inside of the air fryer that has been sprayed with cooking spray. Spread them out as well as possible.
6. Cook 7 minutes, turn and cook another 8 minutes.
7. Remove and repeat with the other two chops.

Ham Steak with Pineapple Glaze

I love grilled pineapple, so it stands to reason that I would love ham steak with air fried pineapple glaze. This is so delicious you will want to eat it until it is gone. You use pineapple, maple syrup and brown sugar to create this glaze from heaven. The recipe serves two requiring a ½ pound ham steak that is about ½ inch thick. You might want to make more than one even though there are still only two to serve because this ham makes the best sandwiches for lunch. You don't even need to put condiments on them.

Ingredients:
¾ cup brown sugar
½ cup apple cider vinegar
½ cup maple syrup
2 tablespoons Dijon mustard
1 teaspoon ground black pepper
2 cups fresh pineapple, cubed
1 ½-pound ham steak, cut in half to fit in the basket

Directions:
1. Mix in a bowl the brown sugar, vinegar, syrup, mustard and pepper to make a glaze. I use a whisk to get it smooth.
2. Preheat the air fryer to 400 degrees F for 5 minutes.
3. Toss the pineapple cubes in the glaze and get just a little on each cube even if it is one side. You need to keep enough to glaze the ham steak too.

4. Place the cubes into a pan that fits inside the air fryer that has been sprayed with cooking spray.
5. Cook for 2 minutes and shake the pan in the basket with tongs and cook 2 more minutes. Shake the pan again and cook for another 3 minutes. Shake the pan and cook 3 more minutes. Pour out the pineapple into a bowl, cover with foil and keep warm.
6. Place the ham steak into the same pan the pineapple was in sprayed with cooking spray. Spread half of what is left of the glaze on the side facing up and cook at 380 degrees F for 10 minutes.
7. Flip the steak over and brush on the rest of the glaze and cook for 8 more minutes.
8. Pour the pineapple cubes on top and cook 2 minutes and serve.

Harvest Citrus and Honey Glazed Ham

This ham is seasoned with all kinds of fall flavored spices like cinnamon, ginger, cloves and more plus honey and brown sugar and a dose of orange juice. It makes for a flavorful ham suitable for 6 to 8 people. I use a fully cooked spiral sliced or pre-sliced ham and it works beautifully.

Ingredients:
½ cup light brown sugar
2 tablespoons orange juice

¼ cup honey

2 tablespoons Dijon mustard

2 tablespoons apple cider vinegar

1 teaspoon orange zest

¼ teaspoon ground ginger

¼ teaspoon ground cloves

¼ teaspoon ground cinnamon

¼ teaspoon smoked paprika

¼ teaspoon salt

¼ teaspoon pepper

2 1/2-pound fully cooked boneless smoked ham

Directions:

1. In a bowl combine the brown sugar, orange juice, honey, Dijon, vinegar, orange zest, ginger, cloves, cinnamon, paprika, salt and pepper and mix well.
2. Preheat the air fryer to 320 degrees F for 5 minutes.
3. Remove the ham from the wrapper and pat it dry.
4. Spray a pan that fits inside the air fryer with cooking spray and place the ham in it.
5. Drizzle about ¼ cup of the glaze over top and spread it out with a brush. Cover the pan with foil and cook for 15 minutes.
6. Remove the pan from the air fryer and set on a heat resistant surface. Carefully remove the foil and brush the top of the ham with glaze.
7. Place the pan with the ham in the air fryer without the foil and cook another 5 minutes at 320 degrees F.
8. Open the drawer and brush with more glaze. Cook 5 more minutes. Do this two more times at 3 minute intervals.
9. Remove the ham from the air fryer, let rest 5 minutes and serve.

Honey Pork Ribs

Sweet with a hint of Asian spice from the five spice powder and teriyaki sauce, these ribs will be the hit of dinner. This recipe calls for ginger paste, which works best, but if you can't find it, grate 1 tablespoon of fresh ginger. The ribs must be marinated overnight and the recipe makes 2 servings.

Ingredients:

1 ½ tablespoon sugar
1/8 teaspoon five spice powder
½ teaspoon ginger paste
½ teaspoon salt
¼ teaspoon pepper
1 tablespoon teriyaki sauce, more if using fresh ginger
1 pound pork ribs, separated from the rack
½ tablespoon tomato sauce
1 tablespoon honey (2 works better for me)
1 tablespoon warm water
1 teaspoon sugar
1 teaspoon olive oil
1 teaspoon garlic, peeled and chopped
1 tablespoon light soy sauce

Directions:

1. Make the marinade by combining the sugar, five spice powder ginger paste, salt, pepper and teriyaki sauce in a bowl. It should be like a thick paste.
2. Place the ribs in the bowl and stir around to coat all of them. Cover and put in the refrigerator overnight.
3. When ready to cook, remove the ribs from the refrigerator.
4. Spray the basket of the air fryer with cooking spray, shake off excess marinade from each rib and place in the basket.
5. Cook at 320 degrees F for 8 minutes. You want them every so slightly under cooked because you must warm them up again.
6. In a bowl, combine the tomatoes sauce, honey, water and sugar and whisk until well combined.
7. In a large skillet over medium heat, sauté the garlic in the oil about 1 to 2 minutes.
8. Add the soy sauce and all the sauce ingredients in the bowl.
9. Bring to a low boil and add all the ribs stirring around to coat them all with the sauce. Cook until heated through and serve.

Italian Style Pork Roast

The flavors of garlic, rosemary, Parmesan and pork make this roast a real thriller. Serve with Alfredo sauce over pasta and some vegetables and you have a delicious meal. This recipe serves 4.

Ingredients:
2 tablespoons olive oil
4 cloves garlic, peeled and minced
1 tablespoon dried rosemary
salt and pepper to taste
2 to 3 pound pork tenderloin
¼ to ½ cup fresh grated Parmesan cheese

Directions:
1. Preheat the air fryer to 360 degrees F for 6 minutes.
2. In a bowl, whisk together the olive oil, garlic, rosemary, salt and pepper. It will be pasty. Spread this on the top and sides of the tenderloin.
3. Spray the basket of the air fryer with cooking spray and place the roast in and cook 25 minutes. Check the temperature of

the roast. It should be about 140 degrees F or a little less. If not, cook a little longer.
4. Sprinkle the Parmesan cheese over the roast and cook another 5 to 8 more minutes but watch so the cheese does not burn.
5. Let the roast sit 5 minutes and then slice and serve.

Maple Glazed Ham

Always use real maple syrup and not the stuff for pancakes you get in the grocery store. Real maple syrup is expensive but worth every penny when it comes to cooking with it. This recipe feeds 6 to 8 people and I use boneless, pre-cooked ham but you if you can fit a bone in ham in your air fryer, go for it.

Ingredients:
5 to 6 pound ham
16 whole cloves
1 ½ cups maple syrup
¼ teaspoon ground nutmeg
¼ teaspoon allspice
½ teaspoon ground ginger
1 can pineapple slices
1 jar maraschino cherries

Directions:
1. Score the ham and stud it with the cloves and place it on a dish.

2. In a bowl, whisk together the maple syrup, nutmeg, all spice and ginger.
3. Pour the glaze over top and let it sit at room temperature 1 hour, basting 4 times during that hour with the glaze that settles on the plate.
4. Preheat the air fryer to 350 degrees F for 5 minutes. Spray the basket with cooking spray.
5. Place the ham in the basket without the plate under it.
6. Cook 1 hour or until the internal temperature reaches 140 degrees F.
7. Decorate the top of the ham with drained pineapple slices and drained cherries in the holes of the pineapple slices.
8. Put back in the air fryer for 5 to 8 minutes just to brown the pineapple.
9. Let rest 5 minutes before slicing.

Parmesan Pork Chops

These chops are crispy and tasty and most of the crunch comes from chopped up pork rinds. I use center cup bone in chops and do two batches of three. Stand the chops on end leaning against the basket to make them fit. If none of them are lying flat you do not have to turn them during the cooking time. This recipe makes 6 pork chops.

Ingredients:
4 to 6 center cut pork chops with bone
½ teaspoon salt

¼ teaspoon pepper

1 cup pork rind crumbs

3 tablespoon grated fresh Parmesan cheese

½ teaspoon onion powder

¼ teaspoon chili powder

1 teaspoon smoked paprika

2 large eggs, beaten

Directions:
1. Preheat the air fryer to 400 degrees F for 8 minutes and spray the basket with cooking spray.
2. Season the chops with salt and pepper on both sides and set aside.
3. Grind the pork rinds in the food processor and pour into a shallow bowl.
4. Add the Parmesan cheese, onion powder, chili powder and paprika and whisk in well.
5. Beat the eggs in another bowl.
6. Dip each chop in the eggs and then in the pork rind mixture and press it in so it sticks.
7. Place three chops in the basket of the air fryer and cook 7 minutes, turn and cook 8 more minutes.
8. Repeat with other three chops and serve.

Paprika Pork Ribs

Spicy and smoky, these ribs are done and ready to eat in half an hour. Serve them with salad and baked beans and you have a great meal for 2.

Ingredients:
1 pound ribs, cut apart so they fit in the air fryer

1 ½ tablespoons paprika

2 ½ tablespoons olive oil

1 teaspoon salt

Directions:
1. Place the ribs in a large bowl.

2. Pour in the paprika, olive oil and salt and stir around or mix with your hands to make sure the ribs are all coated.
3. Spray the basket of the air fryer with cooking spray and place the coated ribs in.
4. Cook at 360 degrees F – Do not preheat the air fryer! Cook for 20 minutes, removing the basket and shaking the ribs around 2 times during that 20 minutes.
5. They should be done and the meat should pull away from the bone.

Sesame Pork Ribs

In this recipe, you make a teriyaki barbeque sauce, which makes more than you need. Keep the left over sauce in the refrigerator for about 2 weeks or freeze it to use later. I cut the ribs to fit in the basket and sometime, depending on the size of the ribs, I must make this in two batches. Never over crowd the air fryer or it won't cook right. This recipe makes 4 servings.

Ingredients:
½ cup soy sauce
2 tablespoons rice vinegar
2 tablespoons honey
2 tablespoons sesame oil
2 tablespoons brown sugar

2 cloves garlic, peeled and minced
1 inch fresh ginger, peeled and grated
¼ cup cold water
1 tablespoon cornstarch
2 pounds baby back ribs
Green onions, thinly sliced for garnish
Sesame seeds for garnish

Directions:
1. Make the sauce in a saucepan by combining the soy sauce, rice vinegar, honey, sesame oil, brown sugar, garlic and ginger. Put it over medium heat and heat until it gets hot.
2. Combine the water and cornstarch and add to the hot sauce. Whisk it in so that there are no lumps and bring it to a simmer. It should thicken and once it does remove it from the heat and set it aside.
3. Preheat the air fryer to 380 degrees F for 6 to 8 minutes.
4. Cut the ribs to be able to fit them into the air fryer basket.
5. Place the ribs in a large bowl with enough of the sauce to coat them well. (I use about 1 cup.
6. Spray the basket of the air fryer with cooking spray and put the ribs in.
7. Cook 15 to 20 minutes or until the meat starts to pull away from the bones.
8. Place the ribs on a platter and brush with a little more of the sauce.
9. Garnish with onions and sesame seed.

Southwestern Style Pork Loin

If you like Southwestern flavors, you will enjoy this pork roast. It has onions, jalapenos, peppers, cilantro and more. I usually serve it with beans and rice for a complete meal.

Ingredients:
½ cup vegetable oil
½ cup green onion tops, chopped
½ cup onion, peeled and chopped
½ cup cilantro, chopped

2 jalapenos, stemmed, seeded and chopped
1 teaspoon chili powder
½ teaspoon cumin
1 teaspoon garlic powder
1 teaspoon coriander
1 teaspoon paprika
1 pinch cayenne pepper
2 pound pork loin roast

Directions:

1. Place the vegetable oil, green onions, regular onion, cilantro and jalapenos in the bowl of a food process and pulse until it creates a paste.
2. In a small bowl combine the chili powder, cumin, garlic powder, coriander, paprika and cayenne.
3. Place the roast in the middle of a square of foil that can be folded over the roast and sealed.
4. Rub the roast down with the chili powder seasoning mix on top and sides.
5. Pour ¾ cup of the paste over top and spread on the top of the roast.
6. Wrap the roast in the foil and put in the air fryer basket.
7. Set for 350 degrees F and cook for 10 minutes.
8. Carefully fold the foil down to expose the very top of the roast.
9. Set for 300 degrees F and cook for 40 more minutes. Check with a meat thermometer to make sure the roast has an internal temperature of 145 degrees F.
10. Remove from the air fryer and carefully unwrap and watch for steam. Let it sit about 10 minutes and slice crosswise in 1/2-inch thick slices.

Takeout Sweet and Sour Pork

One of my favorite Chinese takeout dishes is sweet and sour pork. I enjoy when the pork is breaded with a crispy coating and this recipe does not disappoint. I have split into 2 sections; one for the pork and one for the sweet and sour sauce. I know you will enjoy this recipe if you have a sweet tooth and also like pork. It serves 4 people.

Ingredients for the Sauce:
1 cup pineapple juice
½ cup rice vinegar
½ cup light brown sugar
1 tablespoon low sodium soy sauce
1 tablespoon cornstarch
1 tablespoon canola or peanut oil
1 red bell pepper, stemmed, seeded and cut in 1-inch chunks
1 green bell pepper, stemmed, seeded and cut into 1-inch chunks
½ yellow onion, peeled and cut into 1-inch chunks
1 cup pineapple chunks

Ingredients for Pork:
1 cup potato or corn starch
½ teaspoon sea salt

¼ teaspoon ground black pepper

1 pinch Chinese Five Spice Powder

2 large eggs

1 teaspoon sesame oil

3 tablespoons canola or peanut oil, some in a mist bottle

2 pounds pork, cut into bite size chunks

Directions for the Sauce:

1. In a bowl, whisk the pineapple juice, vinegar, brown sugar, soy sauce and cornstarch until it is well combined and somewhat smooth. It will smooth out and thicken once you heat it up. Set the bowl aside for now.
2. In a skillet, heat the oil and add the bell peppers, onion and pineapple. Stir fry for 2 to 3 minutes until tender crisp.
3. Pour in the sauce and stir until thickened.
4. Remove from heat and set aside.

Directions for Pork:

1. In a bowl, whisk together the potato or cornstarch, salt, pepper and five spice powder and set it aside.
2. In another bowl, beat the eggs with the sesame oil and set it aside.
3. Coat the air fryer basket with the canola or peanut oil.
4. Dip each piece of pork in the potato starch mixture and shake off excess.
5. Dip next into the egg mixture and shake off excess.
6. Dip back into the potato starch mixture and place in the air fryer basket.
7. Do each piece completely and only do what will fit in the air fryer at the time.
8. Spray the pork pieces with canola or peanut oil in a mist bottle.
9. Set for 340 degrees 4 minutes. Shake the basket and cook another 4 minutes. Shake the basket again and cook another 2 to 4 minutes. It is done when the coating is browned and you can hear sizzling.
10. Repeat with rest of pork.
11. Heat up the sauce and serve over top.

The next chapter has everything to do with lamb from roasts to chops and even some lamb burgers. There are recipes from all over the world included as well.

Chapter 9: The Best Lamb Recipes From Around The World

Some of these recipes are suitable for the Easter season if you only have a few people over for that holiday. The recipes run the gambit from lamb cutlets to lamb roasts. There are also some delicious lamb burgers and recipes from around the world from China and from India. There are also several different lamb chop recipes for you and your family or guests to enjoy.

Asian Inspired Sichuan Lamb

This lamb is hot because of the Sichuan peppers, but you can substitute ½ teaspoon of cayenne if you cannot find them. It isn't quite as hot, but it is still good. Marinate the lamb at least 1 hour or overnight. I have done it both ways and since I do not like extremely hot foods, the 1 hour was good enough. It was really hot after an overnight marinade. This recipe serves 4.

Ingredients:
1 ½ tablespoons cumin seed (do not use ground cumin)
1 teaspoon Sichuan peppers or ½ teaspoon cayenne
2 tablespoons vegetable oil
1 tablespoon garlic, peeled and minced
1 tablespoon light soy sauce
2 red chili peppers, seeded and chopped (use gloves)
¼ teaspoon granulated sugar
½ teaspoon salt
1 pound lamb shoulder, cut in ½ to 1-inch pieces
2 green onions, chopped
1 handful fresh cilantro, chopped

Directions:
1. Turn on the burner to medium high on the stove and heat up a dry skillet. Pour in the cumin seed and Sichuan peppers or cayenne and toast until fragrant. Turn off the burner and set aside until they are cool. Grind them in a grinder or mortar and pestle.

2. In a large bowl that will contain the marinade and the lamb, combine the vegetable oil, garlic, soy sauce, chili peppers, granulated sugar and salt. Pour in the cumin/pepper combination and mix well.
3. Using a fork, poke holes in the lamb all over the top and bottom. Place the lamb in the marinade, cover and refrigerate. You can also use a closeable plastic bag.
4. Preheat the air fryer to 360 degrees for 5 minutes.
5. Spray the basket with cooking spray.
6. Remove the lamb pieces from the marinade with tongs or slotted spoon and place in basket of the air fryer in a single layer. You may have to do more than 1 batch.
7. Cook for 10 minutes, flipping over 1 half way through. Make sure the lamb's internal temperature is 145 degrees F with a meat thermometer. Put on a serving platter and repeat with rest of the lamb.
8. Sprinkle the chopped green onions and cilantro over top, stir and serve.

Garlic and Rosemary Lamb Cutlets

These cutlets are deliciously garlic flavored but that is not all. There is mustard, rosemary and honey flavors all mixed together to make a delicious dinner. This dish is marinated but you don't have to do it overnight. Twenty minutes is plenty of time. This recipe serves 2 people.

Ingredients:
2 lamb racks (with 3 cutlets per rack)
2 cloves garlic, peeled and thinly sliced into slivers
2 long sprigs of fresh rosemary, leaves removed
2 tablespoon wholegrain mustard
1 tablespoon honey
2 tablespoons mint sauce (I use mint jelly)

Directions:
1. Trim fat from racks and cut slits with a sharp knife in the top of the lamb. Insert slices of the garlic and rosemary leaves in the slits and set the lamb aside.

2. Make the marinade by whisking the mustard, honey and mint sauce together and brush over the lamb racks. Let marinade in a cool area for 20 minutes.
3. Preheat the air fryer to 360 degrees for about 5 minutes.
4. Spray the basket with cooking spray and place the lamb rack or racks into the basket, propping them up however you can get them in to fit.
5. Cook 10 minutes, open and turn the racks and cook 10 more minutes.
6. Place on a platter and cover with foil to let sit 10 minutes before slicing and serving.

Garlic Sauced Lamb Chops

In this recipe you roast the garlic bulb in the air fryer first and now you know how to roast a garlic bulb. Just squish the softened cloves out on fancy crackers for a treat. The garlic sauce will keep any vampire away and make those that love garlic very happy. This recipe makes 8 lamb chops and serves 4 people.

Ingredients:
1 garlic bulb
1 teaspoon + 3 tablespoons olive oil
1 tablespoon fresh oregano, chopped fine
¼ teaspoon ground pepper
½ teaspoon sea salt
8 lamb chops

Directions:

1. Preheat the air fryer to 400 degrees F 5 minutes and while it is preheating take excess paper from the garlic bulb.
2. Coat the garlic bulb with the 1 teaspoon of olive oil and drop it in the basket that has treated with cooking spray. Roast for 12 minutes.
3. Combine the 3 tablespoons of olive oil, oregano, salt and pepper and lightly coat the lamb chops on both with the resulting oil. Let them sit at room temperature for 5 minutes.
4. Remove the garlic bulb from the basket and if it is cool, preheat again to 400 degrees for 3 minutes.
5. Spray the basket with cooking oil and place 4 chops in cooking at 400 degrees F for 5 minutes. Place them on a platter and cover to keep them warm while you do the other chops.
6. Squeeze each garlic clove between the thumb and index finger into a small bowl.
7. Taste and add salt and pepper and mix. Serve along the chops like serving ketchup.

Herb Encrusted Lamb Chops

Coriander and any of the Mediterranean herbs go well with lamb. This recipe has oregano, thyme, rosemary and coriander in it and gives the meat a lovely flavor. Many people like their lamb chops medium rare, but always check the internal temperature. It should never be less than 145 degrees F. One pound of chops can feed 2 people.

Ingredients:

1 teaspoon oregano
1 teaspoon coriander
1 teaspoon thyme
1 teaspoon rosemary
½ teaspoon salt
¼ teaspoon pepper
2 tablespoons lemon juice
2 tablespoons olive oil
1 pound lamb chops

Directions:

1. In a closeable bag, combine the oregano, coriander, thyme, rosemary, salt, pepper, lemon juice and olive oil and shake well so it mixes.
2. Place the chops in the bag and squish around so the mixture is on them. Refrigerate 1 hour.
3. Preheat the air fryer to 390 degrees F for 5 minutes.
4. Place the chops in the basket that has been sprayed with cooking spray.
5. Cook for 3 minutes and pause. Flip the chops over and cook another 4 minutes for medium rare. If you want them more well done cook 4 minutes, pause, turn and cook 5 more minutes.

Herbed Rack of Lamb

I have always thought lamb to have a strong flavor on its own and I'm never real sure If I like it or not. Cooking lamb with herbs tones down that flavor and makes the lamb quite delicious. This recipe is for a rack of lamb that will serve 2 people.

Ingredients:
1 tablespoon olive oil
1 clove garlic, peeled and minced
1 ½ teaspoons fresh ground pepper
1 tablespoon fresh rosemary, chopped
1 tablespoon fresh thyme, chopped
¾ cup breadcrumbs
1 egg
1 to 2 pound rack of lamb

Directions:
1. Place the olive oil in a small dish and add the garlic. Mix well.
2. Brush the garlic on the rack of lamb and season with pepper.
3. In one bowl combine the rosemary, thyme and breadcrumbs and break the egg and whisk in another bowl.
4. Preheat air fryer 350 degrees F for 5 minutes. Spray with cooking spray.
5. Dip the rack in the egg and then place in the breadcrumb mixture and coat the rack.
6. Place rack in air fryer basket and cook 20 minutes.
7. Raise the temperature to 400 degrees F and set for 5 more minutes.
8. Tear a piece of aluminum foil that will fit to wrap the rack. Take it out of the basket with tongs and put it in the middle of the foil. Carefully wrap and let sit about 10 minutes. Unwrap and serve.

Lamb Roast with Root Vegetables

I keep a small tape measure in my purse for when I go to the grocery store. Why, you might ask? So, I can measure pieces of meat that will fit into my air fryer. I know the diameter of my air fryer and I only buy meat that fits or that can be cut to fit. This is one of those times you need to take a tape measure to the meat market. You will need a 3 pound leg of lamb (it can be a little over) for this recipe. I usually have the butcher take the bone out or it would never fit. In this recipe you do the vegetables and the meat in increments. You do the sweet potato wedges first for about 20 minutes and then you do the carrots for another 30 minutes. You keep them as warm as possible and when the meat is done, in about 1 hour 15 minutes, you remove the meat to rest and throw all the veggies back in the air fryer to warm and crisp up. This will feed 4 to 6 people and you don't need to cook anything else.

Ingredients:
4 cloves garlic, peeled and sliced thin, divided
2 springs fresh rosemary, leaves pulled off, divided
3 pound leg of lamb
salt and pepper to taste, divided
2 medium sized sweet potatoes, peeled and cut into wedges
2 tablespoon oil, divided
2 cups baby carrots
1 teaspoon butter
4 large red potatoes, cubed

Directions:
1. Slice the garlic and take the leaves of the rosemary.
2. Cut about 5 to 6 slits in the top of the lamb and insert slices of garlic and some rosemary in each. Salt and pepper the roast to your taste and set aside to cook after the vegetables are done.
3. Coat the sweet potatoes in 1 tablespoon of olive oil and season with salt and pepper.
4. Spray the basket of the air fryer with cooking spray and put in the wedges. You may have to do two batches. Set for 400 degrees F and air fry 8 minutes, shake and cook another 8 minutes or so. Dump into a bowl and cover with foil.
5. Place the carrots in some foil to cover and put the butter on top of them. Enclose them in the foil and place them in the air

fryer. Set for 400 degrees for 20 minutes. Remove from the air fryer.

6. Coat the basket with cooking spray. Mix the red potatoes with the other tablespoon of oil and salt and pepper to taste. Place in the air fryer and cook at 400 degrees F for 20 minutes, shaking after 10 minutes have elapsed.

7. Use a foil tray or baking dish that fits into the air fryer and coat with cooking spray. Place the left over garlic and rosemary in the bottom and place the lamb on top.

8. Set for 380 degrees F and cook 1 hour, checking after 30 minutes and 45 minutes to make sure it isn't getting too done. Increase the heat to 400 degrees F and cook for 10 to 15 minutes.

9. Remove the roast from the air fryer and set on a platter. Cover with foil and rest 10 minutes while you dump all the vegetables back in the basket and cooking at 350 degrees F for 8 to 10 minutes or until heated through.

10. Serve all together.

Lemon and Cumin Coated Rack of Lamb

Lemon and lamb is always delicious together but add cumin and you have a real treat. This recipe calls for about 1 ½ to 1 ¾ pound Frenched rack of lamb. A frenched rack has all the meat up at one end and the ribs are clean hanging down from it. There are usually 8 chops involved. You butcher can do this for you. To French the bones means to expose them. There are several online sources to teach you how to French a rack of lamb and it is not that hard. Give it a try.

Ingredients:
1 ½ to 1 ¾ pound Frenched rack of lamb
Salt and pepper to taste
½ cup breadcrumbs
1 teaspoon cumin seed
1 teaspoon ground cumin
½ teaspoon salt
1 teaspoon garlic, peeled and grated
Lemon zest (1/4 of a lemon)
1 teaspoon vegetable or olive oil
1 egg, beaten

Directions:
1. Season the lamb rack with salt and pepper to taste and set it aside.
2. In a large bowl, combine the breadcrumbs, cumin seed, ground cumin, salt, garlic, lemon zest and oil and set aside.
3. In another bowl, beat the egg.
4. Preheat to air fryer to 250 degrees F for 5 minutes
5. Dip the rack in the egg to coat and then into the breadcrumb mixture. Make sure it is well coated.
6. Spray the basket of the air fryer with cooking spray and put the rack in. You may have to bend it a little to get it to fit.
7. Set for 250 degrees and cook 25 minutes.
8. Increase temperature to 400 degrees F and cook another 5 minutes. Check internal temperature to make sure it is 145 degrees for medium rare or more.
9. Remove rack when done and cover with foil for 10 minutes before separating ribs into individual servings.

Macadamia Rack of Lamb

This is another rack of lamb recipe but it uses macadamia nuts to give flavor and some crunch. It makes enough for 4 people and is very easy to make. Serve with some buttered green beans mixed with some toasted macadamia nuts. It is possible to substitute almonds or pistachios for the macadamia nuts.

Ingredients:
1 tablespoon olive oil
1 clove garlic, peeled and minced
1 ½ to 1 ¾ pound rack of lamb
Salt and pepper to taste
¾ cup unsalted macadamia nuts
1 tablespoon fresh rosemary, chopped
1 tablespoon breadcrumbs
1 egg, beaten

Directions:
1. Mix the olive oil and garlic and brush it all over the rack of lamb. Season with salt and pepper.
2. Preheat the air fryer 250 degrees F for 8 minutes.
3. Chop the macadamia nuts as fine as possible and put them in a bowl.
4. Mix in the rosemary and breadcrumbs and set it aside.
5. Beat the egg in another bowl.
6. Dip the rack in the egg mixture to coat completely.
7. Place the rack in the breadcrumb mixture and coat well.
8. Spray the basket of the air fryer with cooking spray and place the rack inside.
9. Cook at 250 degrees for 25 minutes and then increase to 400 and cook another 5 to 10 minutes or until done.
10. Cover with aluminum foil for 10 minutes, uncover and separate into chops and serve.

Perfect Lamb Burgers

These are not just plain lamb burgers. They are a little more exotic with a Moroccan flair using Moroccan spice blends and Harissa Paste. Find the Harissa paste in the world section of your supermarket and is a lovely blend of different peppers and spices. Make your own Moroccan spice with the recipe below that makes 2 tablespoons of the spice mix, which is a little more than what you need for the lamb burgers and the accompanying dip. Save the rest and use it on chicken or beef. I serve the burgers without a bun and put the dip in small containers so you can dip like it is ketchup. You can put the burgers on a bun and spread the bun with the dip too. This makes 4 burgers.

Ingredients for Moroccan Spice Mix:
1 teaspoon ground ginger
1 teaspoon ground cumin
1 teaspoon sea salt
¾ teaspoon ground black pepper
½ teaspoon ground coriander
½ teaspoon ground allspice
½ teaspoon ground cloves
½ teaspoon ground cinnamon
½ teaspoon cayenne

Ingredients for Burgers and Dip:
1 ½ pound ground lamb
1 teaspoon Harissa paste

2 tablespoons Moroccan spice mix, divided
2 teaspoons garlic, peeled and minced
¼ teaspoon fresh chopped oregano
3 tablespoons plain Greek yogurt
1 small lemon, juiced

Directions for Moroccan Spice Mix:
1. Whisk the ginger, cumin, salt, pepper, coriander, allspice, cloves, cinnamon and cayenne in a small bowl and set aside.

Directions for Burgers and Dip:
1. Place the ground lamb in a bowl and add the Harissa sauce, 1 tablespoon of the homemade Moroccan spice mix, and the garlic. Mix in everything with the hands and form 4 patties.
2. Preheat the air fryer to 360 degrees for 5 minutes while making the patties.
3. Spray the basket of the air fryer with cooking spray and place two of the burgers in.
4. Cook a total of 12 minutes, flipping after 6 minutes.
5. Repeat with the other two burgers.
6. While burgers cook, make the dip by chopping the fresh oregano and placing it in a bowl with the yogurt, 1 teaspoon of the Moroccan spice mix and the juice of the lemon. Whisk this with a fork and divide into small containers to serve with the burgers when they are done.

Simple Yet Tasty Lamb Chops

There are only 6 ingredients to this recipe, but it has wonderful flavors that burst in your mouth. These chops only take 30 minutes to make, so you can have dinner on the table before 6 pm after work. You air fry one clove of garlic, not one head of garlic. I used two cloves because I didn't think one was quite enough.

Ingredients:
1 clove of garlic separated from the head of garlic (maybe 2)
1 ½ tablespoons olive oil
4 lamb chops
½ tablespoon fresh oregano, chopped
Salt and pepper to taste

Directions:
1. Preheat the air fryer to 400 degrees F for 6 minutes.
2. Take a little of the olive oil and coat the garlic clove(s). Place in the basket of the air fryer and roast 12 minutes.
3. While the garlic is cooking, mix the oregano, salt and pepper in a small bowl. Add the rest of the olive oil and mix well.
4. Spread a thin coating of the oregano mixture on both sides of the lamb chops and reserve the rest.

5. Remove the clove(s) of garlic from the basket of the air fryer with rubber tipped tongs. Be careful because the cloves will be very soft and you don't want them to break open quite yet.
6. Spray the basket of the air fryer with cooking spray and place the lamb chops in, 2 at a time in 2 batches. Cook 5 minutes, turn and cook another 4 minutes.
7. When chops are done, squeeze the garlic out of the papery shell into the rest of the oregano mixture and mix it in. Serve this on the side like ketchup.

Tandoori Lamb

This Indian inspired dish uses ginger, cardamom, cinnamon and fennel to name a few. It will get your taste buds standing at attention and make them very happy. Tandoori dishes are usually cooked in a clay conical dish, but this one adapts to the air fryer quite nicely. It makes 4 servings.

Ingredients:
½ onion, peeled and quartered
5 cloves garlic, peeled
4 slices fresh ginger, peeled
1 teaspoon ground fennel
1 teaspoon Garam Masala
1 teaspoon ground cinnamon
½ teaspoon ground cardamom
½ teaspoon cayenne
1 teaspoon salt
1 pound boneless lamb sirloin steaks

Directions:
1. Place the onion, garlic, ginger, fennel, Garam Masala, cinnamon, cardamom, cayenne and salt in a blender and pulse 4 to 6 times until ground.
2. Place the lamb steaks in a large bowl and slash the meat so the spices will permeate into it.
3. Pour the spice mix over top and rub in both sides. Let sit room temperature 30 minutes or cover and refrigerate overnight.
4. Preheat the air fryer to 350 degrees F for 10 minutes.

5. Spray the basket with cooking spray and place lamb steaks in without letting them overlap much. You may have to do this in batches.
6. Cook 7 minutes, turn and cook another 8 minutes.
7. Test with meat thermometer to make sure they are done. Medium well will be 150 degrees F.

Main dishes are now completed in this book and we move on to side dishes. Of course, everyone knows that French fries are great when done in an air fryer and you can make fries with potatoes, sweet potatoes, zucchini and more. There are other sides that are just as delicious and healthier than if they were to be air fried. Wait until you see all the incredible side dishes you can make in an air fryer.

Chapter 10: Amazing Side Dishes

French fries are probably the most popular side to make in an air fryer, but there are so many other options. In this chapter, we will explore all kinds of fries from avocado fries to zucchini fries but will also delve into baked potatoes and other vegetables that can double as main dishes for vegetarians.

Avocado Fries

These fries come out creamy on the inside and crispy on the outside. If you love avocados, you will definitely love these fries. If you do not like Cajun seasoning, you do not have to put it in the recipe. Just mix your bread crumbs with various desired herbs and salt and pepper instead. I have been known to add some Parmesan cheese to the bread crumbs on occasion and it made them even crunchier.

Ingredients:
1 cup panko bread crumbs
½ teaspoon salt
¼ teaspoon pepper
2 eggs, beaten
1 teaspoon Cajun seasoning
2 large avocados, peeled and cut in 8 slices each

Directions:
1. Preheat the air fryer to 380 degrees F for 5 minutes
2. Combine the bread crumbs, salt and pepper in a shallow dish and set it aside.
3. Beat the eggs with the Cajun seasoning and set aside.
4. Prepare the avocado and do only as many slices as you can fit into your air fryer at one time. You will probably have 2 batches.
5. Dip an avocado slice into the egg mixture and shake off excess. Place the slice in the bread crumbs and roll it around so it is completely covered.

6. Spray the basket of the air fryer with cooking spray and place the wedge in the basket. Repeat with other wedges until the basket is full and the wedges are in a single layer.
7. Cook for 3 minutes, turn the wedges and cook another 3 to 5 minutes or until golden brown and have the crunch you desire.
8. Repeat process with the rest of the avocado wedges.

Bacon Cabbage Wedges

You do not know what you are missing until you try this. It is hard to explain the taste and texture. It is crunchy with a smoky cabbage flavor. They are so good. The important part is to keep the core in tact so that the leaves do not fall off. This makes 4 wedges.

Ingredients:
6 strips thick bacon
1 small head cabbage, outer leaves removed, core in tact
1 teaspoon garlic powder
1 teaspoon onion powder
¼ teaspoon red chili flakes
½ teaspoon fennel seed
Salt and pepper to taste
3 tablespoons olive oil

Directions:

1. Spray the air fryer basket with cooking spray and place the bacon in. Air fry at 350 degrees F for 10 minutes. If you don't want to use the air fryer to cook the bacon, do it in a skillet and drain on paper towels.
2. Cut the cabbage in wedges keeping the core intact so the layers stay together. You should come out with 4 to 8 wedges.
3. In a bowl combine the garlic powder, onion powder, chili flakes, fennel, salt and pepper.
4. Drizzle each wedge with oil and sprinkle on both sides with the seasoning mix.
5. Spray air fryer basket with cooking spray and lay wedges in a single layer. You may have to do 2 batches.
6. Cook at 400 degrees F for 6 minutes. Turn the wedges and cook 6 more minutes.
7. Place on a serving dish and sprinkle with the crumbled bacon.

Baked Sweet Potatoes

I think sweet potatoes are sweet enough as they are. I try not to add maple syrup or honey (not even marshmallows) to them because for me, it makes them way too sweet. This is a simple recipe for baked sweet potatoes that is very good. There isn't much too it but it makes a nice side dish. If you want to make it a main dish, add some chopped green onion, bacon and some cheese to sprinkle over top. Parmesan is best in that case.

Ingredients:
3 medium size to small sweet potatoes
1 tablespoon olive oil
1 teaspoon kosher salt

Directions:
1. Poke holes in the potatoes with a fork all the way around. Coat the potatoes with olive oil and sprinkle them with salt.
2. Spray the air fryer basket with cooking spray and place the potatoes in the basket.
3. Cook at 390 for about 40 to 45 minutes. You can tell when they are done if they are soft when poked with a fork again.
4. Remove from the air fryer, slice open and serve with any toppings you desire.

Citrus Parmesan Broccoli Side Dish

Broccoli does go with Parmesan, but I was totally surprised that you could combine citrus flavors with both and it taste good. Not only that, but there are olives in this dish too. If you don't like olives, just leave them out.

Ingredients:
6 cups water
2 pounds broccoli crowns, stemmed cut into 1 inch florets
2 tablespoons olive oil
1 teaspoon kosher salt
¼ teaspoon pepper
½ cup fresh grated Parmesan
2 teaspoons lemon zest
¼ cup pitted and halved Kalamata olives

Directions:
1. Place the water in a saucepan and bring to a boil over high heat.

2. Place the broccoli florets in and cook 4 minutes until tender crisp. Drain well.
3. Toss with the olive oil, salt and pepper to coat.
4. Spray the air fryer basket with cooking spray and place as much of the florets in to make a single layer. You may have to do more than one batch.
5. Set for 400 degrees F and time for 16 minutes total, pausing at 8 minutes to turn and toss broccoli and cooking the other 8 minutes.
6. Place the broccoli in a serving bowl. When it is all done, toss with the Parmesan, lemon zest and olives and serve.

Crunchy Onion Rings

I love onion rings but hate the frozen ones that look uniform and perfect. I like to use Vidalia or Texas sweet onions and hand dip them in a batter and fry them. This recipe makes it easy to make onion rings that way and with less oil too.

Ingredients:
½ cup all-purpose flour
½ teaspoon kosher salt, divided
1 teaspoon smoked paprika
1 large egg
1 tablespoon water
1 cup panko bread crumbs (white or wheat)
1 sweet onion, peeled and cut into rounds

Directions:

1. In a shallow bowl, combine the flour, ¼ teaspoon of the salt and the paprika and set it aside.
2. In another bowl beat the egg with the water and set it aside.
3. In a third dish, combine the remaining ¼ teaspoon of salt with the panko bread crumbs and set aside.
4. Spray the air fryer basket with cooking spray.
5. Take an onion ring and dredge it in the flour mixture shaking off the excess.
6. Dip it in the egg mixture and place directly in the panko mixture making sure it is completely coated.
7. Place in the air fryer. Repeat with other rings until you have, more or less, a single layer of onion rings in the basket.
8. Cook at 380 degrees F for 5 minutes, turn and cook another 5 minutes until golden brown.
9. Repeat with other onion rings.

Fried Fresh Brussels Sprouts

I normally do not like Brussels sprouts but I do like these. The Brussels sprouts get a crunchy texture but they are very flavorful. This recipe makes about 2 servings, but you might want more. You usually can fit 10 of the sprouts in a regular size air fryer. If you do more, you will have to do 2 batches. You can also sprinkle the Brussels sprouts when they are done with cooked, crumbled bacon if you like.

Ingredients:
10 Brussels sprouts

1 tablespoon olive oil
1/4 teaspoon garlic powder
¼ teaspoon onion powder
½ teaspoon salt
¼ teaspoon pepper

Directions:
1. Wash off the Brussels sprouts, drain and pat dry with a clean towel.
2. Cut off the bottom stem and cut the Brussels Sprout in half and put them in a bowl.
3. Add the olive oil, garlic powder, onion powder, salt and pepper and toss to coat.
4. Spray the air fryer basket with cooking spray and place the spouts in a single layer in the basket.
5. Cook at 360 degrees F for 12 minutes, shaking the basket half way through the cooking time. They should be slightly brown and hot when done.
6. Pour into a serving plate. You can squeeze some lemon or lime juice over them or add some cooked bacon or just leave them plain.

Fried Green Tomatoes

This old southern favorite recipe tastes twice as nice when air fried and has less grease. This recipe makes about 6 servings and you will not be able to wait for tomato season to start so you can have them again.

Ingredients:
4 medium to large green tomatoes
Salt and pepper to taste
2 tablespoons milk
2 eggs
1 cup all-purpose flour
2 teaspoons garlic powder, divided
2 teaspoons paprika, divided
½ cup panko bread crumbs
½ cup yellow cornmeal

Directions:
1. Cut the tomatoes into thick slices ¼-inch thick and season with salt and pepper.
2. Whisk the water and eggs in a bowl and set it aside.
3. In a shallow dish combine the flour, 1 teaspoon garlic powder and 1 teaspoon paprika and whisk well. Set this dish aside.
4. In another shallow dish combine the remaining 1 teaspoon garlic powder, remaining teaspoon paprika, bread crumbs and yellow cornmeal.
5. Dredge a slice of tomato in the flour mixture and shake off excess. Dip in the egg mixture and coat both sides with the panko mixture. Place on a wire cooling rack until ready to cook. Repeat with other slices.
6. Spray the air fryer basket with cooking spray and place some of the tomato slices in without overlapping much. Spray the slices in the basket with cooking spray and cook 360 degrees F for 10 minutes. Open the air fryer and flip the slices and cook another 10 minutes.
7. Repeat with all the slices and serve.

Garlic Fried Mushrooms

Normally you would not wash mushrooms in water before you cook them because they suck up the moisture and hold it in. However, when you are going to cook them in an air fryer, it is fine because the heat and wind created by the air fryer makes the moisture in the mushrooms evaporate. Mushrooms and garlic are delicious together and these mushrooms just make that more apparent.

Ingredients:
1 pound button mushrooms
1 heaping tablespoon garlic, peeled and minced fine
1 teaspoon onion powder
¼ teaspoon pepper
2 teaspoons low sodium soy sauce

Directions:
1. Pour mushrooms into a colander and run water over them. Rinse well and drain. Put them in a bowl and cover with water. Swish around with the hands and drain into the colander again.
2. Dry bowl and once mushrooms have drained, place them back in with the garlic, onion powder, pepper and soy sauce. Mix well.
3. Spray the basket of the air fryer and pour the mushrooms in. You don't have to worry if they are in a single layer or not.
4. Cook at 360 degrees F for 20 minutes. Do not stir or shake during the cooking time.
5. Pour into a serving dish.

Garlic Green Beans with Rosemary

These green beans will be loved by everyone. I use my 6-inch cake pan inside the basket of the air fryer to make sure the basket doesn't get really messy and I don't lose any garlic between the basket and the pan. The beans are still tender but crisp when you eat them and they are flavored with garlic and herbs. Never use frozen or canned green beans in this recipe. It is only good for fresh green beans.

Ingredients:
1 pound fresh green bean, snapped (you can make them bite size or leave them long)
1 ½ tablespoon garlic, peeled and minced
½ teaspoon dried thyme
½ teaspoon dried parsley
½ teaspoon dried oregano
1 teaspoon dried rosemary
½ teaspoon kosher salt
Olive oil in a spray bottle

Directions:
1. Preheat air fryer to 400 degrees F for 5 minutes.
2. Place the green beans into a pan that fits inside the basket of the air fryer. Make sure to spray it with a little olive oil.
3. Sprinkle the garlic over top of the beans.
4. In a little bowl, whisk the thyme, parsley, oregano, rosemary and salt. Sprinkle it over the top of the beans and take hands and toss beans so that they are well coated.
5. Place the pan in the air fryer basket and spray generously with the olive oil spray.
6. Cook a total of 8 minutes, shaking 2 times during the cooking.

Honey Roasted Baby Carrots

This side dish has the flavor of roasted carrots with a touch of sweetness even the kids in the family will love. I use baby carrots but if you grow your own carrots in your backyard, just use them, peel them and cut into bite size pieces. It works just as well. I would use a pan that fits inside the air fryer basket just because the honey is so messy. It is much easier to clean a pan than the basket.

Ingredients:
3 cups baby carrots
1 tablespoon honey
1 tablespoon olive oil
Salt and pepper to taste

Directions:
1. Place the carrots in a bowl and top with the honey and olive oil.
2. Sprinkle with salt and pepper and toss to coat all the carrots.
3. Place in the air fryer and cook at 250 degrees F for 12 minutes. Do not turn or shake.
4. Carrots should be browned and tender crisp when done.

Loaded Baked Potatoes in an Air Fryer

I like to use Yukon Gold potatoes to make loaded baked potatoes because they are already buttery flavored but you can also use russet potatoes. This makes 8 small potatoes, but you can change to use 4 larger potatoes, keep the other ingredients the same and have a larger portion. We eat these for the entre for dinner sometimes.

Ingredients:
4 to 8 potatoes
1 teaspoon olive oil
3 to 4 bacon slices
1 tablespoon butter
3 tablespoons sour cream
1 ½ tablespoons green onions or chives, chopped fine
½ teaspoon salt
¼ teaspoon pepper
¼ cup shredded cheddar

Directions:
- Poke a few holes in the potatoes with a form and coat the unpeeled potatoes with the olive oil. Place in the air fryer and cook 350 degrees F about 20 to 25 minutes or until tender when poked with a fork.
- Let cool 10 to 15 minutes.
- While cooking the potatoes, cook the bacon and drain on paper towels. Crumble when it cools.

- Cut open the potato and remove the potato pulp to a bowl. Keep the skins.
- Combine the potato pulp with butter and sour cream. I use a fork to squish it all in well. If the mixture is a little dry, add more sour cream.
- Sprinkle in the green onions or chives, salt and pepper and mix well.
- Add half of the shredded cheese and half of the bacon and mix in.
- Spoon the potato mixture back into the skins of the potatoes and replace in your air fryer. I like to use a pan that fits in the air fryer because it is easier to handle with the floppy skins.
- Cook at 350 degrees F for 5 to 10 minutes just to get the potatoes hot again.
- Add the rest of cheese and bacon on top of each potato and cook another 4 minutes to melt the cheese. Remove and serve.

Parmesan Garlic Red Potatoes

These tasty little potatoes make a great side dish for just about anything. I love red potatoes to begin with because of their flavor and because they do not need to be peeled. I suggest you use a baking dish that fits inside the air fryer basket for this dish because the olive oil and butter will run through the basket to the bowl below and you want it to stay in with the potatoes to get the full effect from them.

Ingredients:
3 pounds red potatoes
2 tablespoons unsalted butter, melted
2 tablespoon olive oil
4 cloves garlic, peeled and minced
1 teaspoon dried thyme
1 tablespoon dried parsley
½ teaspoon dried oregano
½ teaspoon salt
¼ teaspoon pepper
1/3 cup fresh grated Parmesan cheese

Directions:

1. Cut potatoes in quarters and place in a large bowl and pour the melted butter and olive oil over top.
2. Add the thyme, parsley, oregano, salt and pepper and stir in to coat.
3. Add the parmesan and stir in well.
4. Spray a baking dish that fits into the air fryer basket with cooking oil and pour the potatoes in.
5. Set for 400 degrees F and cook for 20 minutes stirring them around after 10 minutes have elapsed.

Plain Old French Fries

This is a no frills plain old French fry recipe. I use Yukon golds or russets to make them. There is another recipe in this chapter for sweet potato fries. When you put them in the air fryer it is very important to put the fries in a single layer or they will not get crispy wherever they are lying on one another. You will have to do batches. I cover the finished ones with foil and put them in a 250 degree F oven to keep them warm and then when all are done, I put them all in the air fryer at the end and warm everything up to crisp them again for about 4 or 5 minutes.

Ingredients:

2 medium potatoes
2 teaspoons olive oil

¼ teaspoon garlic powder
½ teaspoon kosher salt
¼ teaspoon pepper

Directions:
1. Preheat the air fryer to 380 degrees F for 8 minutes.
2. Peel and cut the potatoes lengthwise in about ¼-inch thin slices and then each slice into ¼-inch fries.
3. Place them in a bowl and add the olive oil, garlic powder, salt and pepper. Mix with hands to make sure all the fries are coated.
4. Place as many fries as you can to make a single layer in the cooking sprayed basket of the air fryer. Use tongs because it is preheated and will be hot.
5. Cook 15 minutes, stopping after 7 or 8 minutes and turning the fries and cooking the rest of the time.
6. The fries should be golden brown and crisp when done.

Roasted Fresh Corn on the Cob

This is a great way to make corn on the cob and it even gets a little brown as if you were really roasting it over a fire. You may have to cut the ears of corn in half to get them into the basket and you might have to do two batches.

Ingredients:
4 ears fresh corn
3 teaspoons vegetable oil or butter

Salt and pepper to taste
A little garlic powder (optional)

Directions:
1. Remove the husks and hair from the corn and wash. Pat dry with a paper towel and cut corn to fit.
2. Drizzle the vegetable oil or melted butter over the corn and sprinkle with salt pepper and garlic powder, if desired.
3. Place the corn in the basket of the air fryer and cook at 400 degrees F for 10 minutes turning once at mid-point.

Squash and Carrot Medley

This recipe uses summer squash and carrots to make a great and healthy side dish. You can even add a few cherry tomatoes cut in half if you like. I eat this as a vegetarian main dish sometimes and it is very filling. Use a baking pan inside the air fryer basket to minimize mess. You cook the carrots longer because they take a little longer to become tender.

Ingredients:
½ pound carrots, peeled and cut in 1 inch slices
6 teaspoons olive oil, divided
1 pound yellow summer squash, ends trimmed and cut into ¾-inch half moons
1 pound zucchini, ends trimmed and cut into ¾-inch half moons
¼ teaspoon ground black pepper
1 tablespoon fresh tarragon leaves (you can use basil, oregano or thyme instead if you like)
1 teaspoon kosher salt

Directions:
1. Spray the baking pan you will be putting into the air fryer basket with cooking spray and put the carrot pieces in along with 2 teaspoons of the olive oil. Toss to coat the carrots.
2. Set the temperature to 400 degrees F and cook 5 minutes.
3. Place the cut squash and zucchini in a large bowl and combine with the remaining olive oil. Sprinkle over the salt and pepper and coat evenly.

4. Add the squash and zucchini and cook for 30 minutes stopping and shaking the basket at least 2 times during the process so everything browns evenly.
5. Sprinkle over the tarragon and serve.

Succulent Sweet Potato Fries

Hands down, this is my favorite recipe in the book. I love sweet potato fries and when you put a little paprika on them and serve them with barbeque sauce, they are absolutely luscious. Not only that, but they are so easy to make it is laughable. Just like the plain fries, you cannot overlap the strips of potato or they won't cook right. Therefore, you do them in batches and keep the first batch warm while cooking the second. Then you pile them all in the air fryer at the end and warm them all up before serving.

Ingredients:
2 medium sweet potatoes, peeled and cut into small wedges or sticks
1 tablespoon olive oil
¼ teaspoon sea salt
¼ teaspoon pepper
2 shakes of smoked paprika
¼ teaspoon garlic powder (optional)

Directions:
1. Peel and cut the potatoes and put them in a large bowl.
2. Pour in the olive oil, salt pepper, paprika and garlic powder and use your hands to mix it up making sure all the potatoes are coated.

3. Preheat the air fryer to 400 degrees F and spray with cooking spray when done.
4. Place enough of the fries in to cover the bottom of the basket.
5. Cook 7 minutes, stop and use tongs to turn the fries over and cook another 14 or 15 minutes or until crisp.
6. Repeat with rest of potatoes.

Zucchini Fries

Yes, you can make fries with zucchini and they are delicious. I like these better than potato fries but not as much as sweet potato fries. They are bulkier than the other fries because you bread the zucchini sticks. This is one way to get kids to eat vegetables. I serve them with ketchup but they are really good dipping in BBQ sauce.

Make Carrot Fries the same way, but par boil the carrots until they are slightly soft before breading and air frying.

Ingredients:
2 medium sized zucchini
1/3 cup parmesan cheese
1 cup plain bread crumbs (Panko makes them a little too crunchy)
¼ teaspoon salt
¼ teaspoon pepper
¼ cup butter

Directions:

1. Peel the skin off the zucchini or not (the bread crumb mixture sticks on better if you do peel them).
2. Cut the zucchini in half and then in half longways too. You have four wedges of zucchini. Cut the wedges into a few wedges long-wise. (4-inches by ½-inch). Trim the seeds out of the centers.
3. Place the parmesan, bread crumbs, salt and pepper in a bowl.
4. Melt the butter in another bowl.
5. Dip each zucchini piece in the butter and then in the breadcrumbs.
6. Place the zucchini pieces in the basket of the air fryer that has been sprayed with olive oil or cooking spray. Do not overlap.
7. Cook 350 degrees F for 20 minutes and keep the first batch warm while cooking the second batch.

Now the fun part! The next chapter finishes up the meal with some sweets and treats that the whole family and guests will love and you won't believe what you can make in an air fryer.

Chapter 11: Desserts, Sweets and Other Treats

Air fryers are truly versatile because you can make so many things in them including appetizers, main dishes, sides and desserts and sweet treats. This chapter focuses on those sweet things in life. I love being able to make a cake, pie, cookies or other dessert without having to turn my oven on in the summer. The air fryer does not pump hot air into the kitchen like the oven does and I get perfect results at, often times, less time. Enjoy the following sweet treats made in your air fryer, however, remember that the air fryer isn't going to make these recipes healthier for you. They will still contain sugar and many calories so go easy on them.

Apple Dumplings

My grandmother used to make apple dumplings when I came over and hers were delicious. These are a little different because grandma made pie dough and this recipe uses puff pastry, but it is still very good and tasty. Since I love cinnamon, my grandma used to use the raisins and brown sugar but also put in 3 or 4 little red heart cinnamon candies in the apple core. If you like cinnamon, I suggest you try that too because it makes the apple dumpling taste much like a candied apple. This recipe makes 2 apple dumplings.

Ingredients:
2 small apples

1 tablespoon brown sugar

2 tablespoon s raisins (I like the golden ones)

2 sheets puff pastry

2 tablespoons butter, melted

Directions:

1. Preheat air fryer to 360 degrees F for 6 minutes.
2. Core the apples and peel 2 strips leaving the skin in the middle around the circumference of the apple.
3. In a small bowl mix the brown sugar and raisins and stuff it equally into the area where the core of the apple was.
4. Place each apple on one of the puff pastry sheets and fold the puff pastry around the apple to completely cover it.
5. Place the covered apples in a cooking spray covered baking pan that fits inside the air fryer.
6. Brush each covered apple with melted butter.
7. Bake for 25 minutes, turning them 1 once until the dumpling is golden brown and the apple is soft inside. Poke it with a skewer to make sure.
8. Let cool 10 minutes before serving.

Apple Empanadas

This Latin-inspired dessert dish uses apples, spices and honey to make a delicious filling for empanada wrappers. You can also make them a little smaller by using won ton wrappers. This makes 12 empanada size sweet empanada. Serve with whipped cream and a sprinkle of cinnamon.

Ingredients:

2 apples, peeled and diced

1 teaspoon cinnamon

1/8 teaspoon nutmeg

1 teaspoon vanilla

2 tablespoons honey

2 teaspoon cornstarch

1 teaspoon water

11 empanada wrappers

Directions:

1. Peel and core the apples and dice them. Place them in a medium sauce pan over medium high heat.
2. Add the cinnamon, nutmeg, vanilla and honey and cook about 3 minutes until the apples soften.
3. Combine the cornstarch and water in a small bowl and whisk well. Add to the apple mixture and cook 30 seconds. Remove the pan from the heat.
4. Lay an empanada wrapper on a flat service and spoon some of the apple mixture onto the wrapper and spread it out. Roll it in half and pinch along the edges. Roll each side inward and twist until closed.
5. Spray the air fryer basket with butter flavored cooking spray. Place the empanadas inside. It is fine if they overlap, put them all in.
6. Set the air fryer to 400 degrees F and cook 8 minutes. Flip and turn the empanadas with tongs and cook another 8 to 10 minutes or until golden brown.
7. Cool 8 minutes before serving or eat them cold.

Blondie Bars Using Refrigerated Chocolate Chip Cookie Dough

This is a good recipe for amending store bought, refrigerated chocolate chip cookie dough. You will need a pan that fits inside the air fryer and some parchment paper. You also need aluminum foil to make a sling so you can lift the pan out of the air fryer when it is done by folding it in a long strip, placing the middle of the strip in the air fryer basket and bringing both sides up the sides. Place the pan on top of the strip when you put it in the air fryer with the ends up so you can grab them.

Ingredients:
1 16-ounce package of chocolate chip cookie dough
1 egg
¼ cup vegetable oil
½ cup sugar
¼ cup all-purpose flour
¼ cup cocoa powder
½ teaspoon salt
½ teaspoon baking powder

Directions:

1. Preheat the air fryer to 350 degrees F for 5 minutes.
2. Prepare your cake pan by cutting a piece of parchment paper that fits in the bottom and spraying it with cooking spray. Also fold the foil and position the sling in the air fryer once preheating is done. Just lay it over the basket and when you insert the pan it will go down in.
3. Press the cookie dough into the bottom of the pan and put in the air fryer. Cook for 8 minutes.
4. Meanwhile, prepare the rest of the blondies by combining the eggs, oil and sugar in a bowl, whisking until well combined.
5. In another bowl combine the flour, cocoa, salt and baking powder and whisk well.
6. Gradually add the dry ingredients to the egg mixture folding it in until each addition is incorporated well. I use a rubber spatula. Do not over mix.
7. Open the air fryer when the alarm goes off and pour the dough over the cooked cookie dough.
8. Air fry 15 minutes. Remove immediately with the sling to a rack and cool 10 minutes.
9. Cut into wedges.

Boxed Brownies

Making brownies from a box mix saves time and is much easier. This is how to make brownies in an air fryer. Mix up the batter and divide it between 2 pans that fit inside the air fryer basket. I used 6-inch round cake pans and it worked well.

Ingredients:
1 box brownie mix
The ingredients needed on the box (oil, water etc.)

Directions:
1. Prepare brownies per the instructions on the back of the box.
2. Spray the pan you are using with cooking spray (I used butter flavor) and cut a piece of parchment paper to fit the bottom of the pan and up the sides. The spray will keep the paper in place, but also spray the top of the paper.
3. Pour the brownies into one of each pan, dividing it equally. Some brownie mixes will make enough for 2 pans and some might only make enough for one pan.
4. Set the air fryer for 350 degrees and set for 15 minutes. Check every 5 minutes to make sure the edges are not burning. It might take more or less time depending on your air fryer and the thickness of the brownies.
5. Repeat with the second pan if there is one.
6. Let cool before removing the pan from the air fryer.

Cake Mixes in an Air fryer

Here is another recipe using a boxed mix and these come out very well too. Just make the cake in 2 cake pans that fit into the basket of the air fryer, let cool and frost with your favorite icing. You will need 2 pans and I use two 6-inch round pans.

Ingredients:
1 cake mix
The ingredients needed to make the cake that are on the box.

Directions:

1. Make the cake mix per the directions on the back of the box.
2. Spray a cake pan that fits into the air fryer basket with butter flavored cooking spray.
3. Divide the prepared cake mix between two pans and put one into the air fryer.
4. Set for 330 degrees F and cook for 20 minutes. Check after 10 and after 15 to make sure it is not getting too brown or burned on the edges. Every air fryer is different.   Check to see if it is done by inserting a sharp knife in the center of the cake. If the knife comes out clean, it is done. If there is gooey residue on the knife, it needs more time in the air fryer.
5. Let the cake cool a few minutes and remove from the air fryer. Repeat with the other cake pan.
6. Cool and frost as you like.

Chocolate Cake in an Air Fryer

This is a from scratch cake made in your air fryer. It is dense and delicious and is made in 2 round cake pans that can fit inside the basket of your air fryer. You may never make a cake in your oven again after tasting this chocolaty treat.

Ingredients:
1 stick unsalted butter, room temperature
3 eggs
2/3 cup sugar

½ cup sour cream
1 cup flour
1/3 cup cocoa powder
1 teaspoon baking powder
½ teaspoon baking soda
¼ teaspoon salt
2 teaspoons vanilla

Directions:
1. In a mixing bowl with an electric mixer, whip the butter and add the sugar. Beat in well.
2. Add the eggs and sour cream and beat well.
3. In another bowl combine the flour, cocoa powder, baking powder, baking soda and salt. Gradually add to the wet ingredients while beating.
4. Add the vanilla and mix in well.
5. Spray the cake pans that fit into the basket of the air fryer and evenly divide the batter into each.
6. Preheat the air fryer to 320 degrees F for 8 minutes.
7. Drop one cake pan into the basket and cook 25 minutes. When alarm goes off, check to see if it is done. If so, let sit about 4 to 5 minutes and remove carefully from air fryer. Replace with the other pan and cook.
8. Let cool, remove from pans and frost.

Chocolate Chip Cookies

This recipe makes about 9 cookies and you must do them in batches. They come out very soft and delicious. You can even freeze the dough and take out one or two to do in the air fryer on demand.

Ingredients:
1/2 cup butter
¼ cup brown sugar, packed
2 tablespoons honey
1 tablespoon milk
1 ¾ cup flour
½ teaspoon baking powder

½ cup chocolate chips

Directions:
1. Preheat the air fryer to 350 degrees F for 5 minutes.
2. Mix the butter with the brown sugar with an electric mixer.
3. Add the honey and milk and mix well.
4. In a bowl mix the flour and baking powder and gradually add the flour at low speed.
5. Add the flour mixture to the wet mixture slowly.
6. Stir in the chocolate chips.
7. Place a piece of foil in the bottom of the air fryer that just fits in the bottom. Spray with cooking spray.
8. Scoop the dough in a tablespoon and roll in a ball. Place 2 in the basket on top of the foil and press down to flatten a little.
9. Cook for 6 minutes.
10. Reduce to 330 degrees F and cook another 2 minutes.
11. Let sit 5 minutes and remove from air fryer with a spatula.
12. Repeat with other cookies.

Double Crust Apple Pie

When you make pie in the air fryer, the crust gets super crispy and delicious but the filling gets almost creamy and smooth with some chunks in it. I use my 6-inch round cake pan that fits in the air fryer basket to make pie, but you might be able to find a small pie pan that will fit. I would stay away from foil pans because if the ingredients are not heavy enough, the pan will flip up and dump the ingredients all over the air fryer basket. Metal or glass pans tend to stay put.

Ingredients:
1 double refrigerated pie crust
1 large apple, peeled, cored and chopped
2 teaspoons lemon juice
2 tablespoons sugar
1 tablespoon ground cinnamon
½ teaspoon vanilla
1 tablespoon butter
1 egg, beaten
Extra sugar or raw sugar

Directions:
1. Let crust come to room temperature and unroll it. Cut both crusts ¼ inch larger than the pan you are putting it in.
2. Spray the pan with cooking spray and place one crust in pressing it against the edges of the pan. Poke a few holes in the bottom with a fork.
3. In a bowl, combine the apples, lemon juice, sugar, cinnamon and vanilla. Mix well to coat all the apples.
4. Pour the apple mixture into the pan over the crust.
5. Cut the butter in pieces and place it on top of the apple mixture.
6. Cover with the second pie crust, cut slits in the top crust and crimp the edges.
7. Preheat the air fryer to 400 degrees F for 5 minutes.
8. Brush the beaten egg over the top crust with a pastry brush.
9. When the air fryer is heated up, carefully place the pie in the basket. Cook at 320 degrees F for 30 minutes.

Note: I make a sling with a piece of heavy duty foil folding it several times to make a 1-inch strip that goes on the bottom of the air fryer basket and up the sides. When I place the pie in, I put it on top of the foil sling with the ends coming up the side of the basket and long enough I can get ahold of it on each side with a pot holder. When done, I pull on the ends and the pie comes up so you can get it out of the basket without burning your hands.

Easy Cherry Pie

You make this just like the apple pie but use cherry pie filling instead of apples. I add a little bit of cinnamon and ginger, but if you do not like spicy cherries, just omit them.

Ingredients:
2 refrigerator pre-made crusts
2 – 21-ounce cans cherry pie filling
1 teaspoon cinnamon
½ teaspoon ground ginger
1 egg beaten

Directions:
1. Let the refrigerator crusts get to room temperature and roll them out. Cut the crusts about ½ inch larger than the size of your pie dish.
2. Spray the pie pan with cooking spray.
3. Lay one of the crusts in the pie pan and press on the bottom and up the sides and poke holes in the bottom with a fork.
4. Mix the cherry pie filling with the cinnamon and ginger and pour into the pie pan on top of the crust.

5. Take the other crust and lay it over top. Crimp the edges and make slits in the top so steam can escape.
6. Brush the top with the beaten egg.
7. Preheat the air fryer to 400 degrees for 5 minutes.
8. Set the pie dish into the basket of the air fryer (see apple pie to learn how to make a foil sling to get the pie out without burning your hands).
9. Reduce the temperature to 320 degrees and cook for 10 minutes. Check the pie to make sure it is not burning. It should have steam coming out of the slits when it is done. If it is not done, put in at 4 minute intervals until it is.

Easy Cheesecake In An Air Fryer

New York Cheesecake is a very dense and heavy cheesecake made with sour cream and cream cheese. This cheesecake uses both sour cream and cream cheese but is a little lighter than a New York type of cheesecake and you might even like it better. It is made in an air fryer and does require a spring form pan that fits into the basket. Spring form pans have a bottom and a side that clamps into place. This makes it easy to get the cheesecake out of the pan because you remove the sides. An 8-inch will not fit in my air fryer but I was able to find a 6-inch and that fits just right.

Ingredients:
2 tablespoons unsalted butter
½ cup graham cracker crumbs

1 tablespoon sugar

2 eggs

¾ cup sugar

½ teaspoon vanilla

2 tablespoons sour cream

15-ounce block cream cheese, at room temperature (this is 2 8-ounce blocks with 1 ounce cut off one of them)

Directions:

1. Preheat the air fryer to 350 degrees F for 4 minutes.
2. Melt the butter.
3. In a bowl combine the graham cracker crumbs and the sugar and mix well. Add the melted butter and mix with a fork.
4. Spray the bottom of the spring form pan with cooking spray and then dump the graham cracker crumb mixture in. Use your hands to flatten it to the bottom of the pan.
5. Make a foil sling by folding a long strip of foil and placing it on the bottom of the air fryer basket so it comes up both sides. Place the spring form pan over the foil sling in the air fryer basket so the two ends are easy to grab.
6. Cook the crust for 4 minutes while making the cheesecake filling.
7. Place the eggs in a mixing bowl and beat with the ¼ cup sugar.
8. Add the vanilla and beat in until frothy.
9. Add the sour cream and cream cheese and beat until smooth and creamy.
10. Pour into the spring form pan without taking out of the air fryer.
11. Place a piece of foil over top of the spring form pan. You will have to wear protective pot holders because the pan will be hot from cooking the crust. Do as best you can to crimp the foil to the edges so it will stay there. It will tend to fly up because of the hot wind created in the air fryer. I tuck mine down deep into the air fryer using silicone gloves. When done, use a sharp knife to cut an "X" in the foil laying on top of the cheesecake.
12. Cook 9 minutes, open the foil a bit and if the cake jiggles like it is liquid in the middle, put it back on for 1 to 2 minutes and check again.

13. Remove from air fryer using the foil sling and cool before serving.

Fruity Mug Cakes

Make these interesting cakes in small size mugs. You will be able to fit 2 in the air fryer at once, so you will have to make 4 in 2 batches. The fruit part is juicy and sweet. This is more like a thick cobbler in a mug, and it is certainly delicious.

Ingredients:
4 plums
1 small pear
1 small peach
1 small apple
1 handful blueberries
1/3 cup brown sugar
1 tablespoon honey
1 cup all-purpose flour
½ cup butter, room temperature
¼ cup sugar
¼ cup Old Fashion Oats

Directions:
1. Core, peel and remove stones from all the fruit and dice in small pieces.
2. Spray each mug with cooking spray and place the fruit in the bottom, spreading evenly between the 4 mugs. Sprinkle each with the brown sugar and top with honey, divided evenly between the 4 mugs.
3. In a bowl combine the flour, butter and sugar and use knives or a pastry mixer to mix until it looks like breadcrumbs.
4. Add the oats and stir in.
5. Cover the tops of the mugs by crumbling in the flour mixture evenly between the 4 mugs.
6. Preheat the air fryer to 320 degrees F for 5 minutes.
7. Place 2 mugs in and cook for 10 minutes. Increase the heat to 380 degrees and cook 5 more minutes.
8. Repeat with other 2 mugs.

9. Cool 5 minutes before serving.

Gooey Lava Cake

Make these lava cakes in regular ramekins. These require baker's sugar, not regular or powdered sugar. You should be able to find this type of sugar in specialty stores. You also need self-rising flour. Don't try to use all-purpose because the cakes will be flatter than a pancake. This makes 4 cakes.

Ingredients:
3 ½ ounces dark chocolate (either pieces or chopped)
3 ½ ounces unsalted butter
2 eggs
3 ½ tablespoons Baker's sugar

Directions:
1. Spray the ramekins with cooking spray and flour the insides.
2. Preheat the air fryer to 375 degrees F for 5 minutes.
3. In a microwave safe bowl, melt the chocolate with the butter at 70% for 3 minutes, stirring every few seconds. Remove and stir to a smooth consistency.
4. In a bowl, whisk the eggs with the sugar until it is frothy and light yellow in color.
5. Pour the chocolate into the eggs and whisk vigorously so the eggs don't start to cook.

6. Once the mixture is well combined, add the flour and use a spatula to fold in everything so it is evenly mixed.
7. Fill ramekins ¾ full and place in the air fryer for 10 minutes. You might be able to get all four in at one time, but if not, just do two at a time.
8. Cook for 10 minutes and remove. Let cook for 2 minutes.
9. Carefully turn the ramekins upside down individually on a plate and tap the bottom with a butter knife. The cake should release to the plate and be dark and gooey.
10. Serve with ice cream on top.

Lemon Pound Cake

My mom always made pound cake when I was a kid but you don't see it around much anymore. The cake got its name because you used a pound of butter, pound of flour, pound of eggs and so on in making the batter. The cake was usually made in a loaf pan and did not rise as much as regular cake. It is also a very dense cake, but extremely flavorful. This one is a lemon cake that is so lemony it will make you pucker, but it is still sweet. Make it in a loaf pan that fits into your air fryer basket. I use foil loaf pans because the batter is heavy and keeps the foil pan from flipping up during cooking. The pan must have a 6 cup capacity and a Bundt pan will work well too.

Ingredients:
¾ cup all-purpose flour
¼ teaspoon salt

½ teaspoon baking powder
1 stick butter (1/2 cup)
1 cup sugar
2 eggs
2 teaspoons vanilla extract
¼ cup lemon juice
1 cup powdered sugar
4 tablespoons lemon juice

Directions:
1. Preheat the air fryer to 3530 degrees F for 10 minutes.
2. Grease and flour the loaf or Bundt pan and set it aside.
3. In a bowl, whisk together the flour, salt and baking powder and set it aside.
4. In a mixing bowl, cream the butter with the sugar.
5. Add eggs, one at a time and mix in.
6. Add the vanilla.
7. Keep the mixer at a low speed and alternate the flour mixture with the ¼ cup of lemon juice until all are incorporated into the mixture and the batter is smooth and creamy.
8. Pour the batter in the pan and bake in the air fryer about 30 to 45 minutes. Check at 30 minutes and if a knife inserted in the center comes out clean, it is done.
9. Cool 15 minutes and turn the cake out onto a plate.
10. Mix the powdered sugar with the 4 tablespoons lemon juice to make a glaze and pour over the pound cake.

Luscious Lemon Cookies

These lemon cookies are outrageously lemony and delicious. They are made with lemon pudding and iced with lemon icing. This makes about 1 dozen small size cookies in the air fryer. You do have to refrigerate the dough 3 hours or overnight and you can freeze the dough and just make what you want when you want. I slice the cookie dough into individual pieces and freeze them that way between wax paper.

Ingredients:
½ cup unsalted butter at room temperature

½ cup sugar

1 3.4-ounc package instant lemon pudding mix

1 teaspoon lemon zest

1 large egg

2 tablespoons milk

1 ½ cups all-purpose flour

1 teaspoon baking powder

¼ teaspoon salt

2/3 cup powdered sugar

2 to 4 teaspoons fresh lemon juice

Directions:

1. In a mixer bowl combine the butter and sugar and cream well. Add the lemon pudding mix and lemon zest and mix well.
2. Add the egg and milk and mix in.
3. In another bowl combine the flour, baking powder and salt. Gradually add to the pudding mixture beating slowly until all is incorporated.
4. Divide the dough in half and on a lightly floured surface roll each half into a 6-inch long roll. Wrap both in plastic wrap or wax paper and put in the refrigerator for at least 3 hours. It will become hard.
5. Preheat the air fryer to 325 degrees F for 4 minutes.
6. Unwrap the dough and cut into ½ inch coin-like slices.
7. Line the bottom of the air fryer basket with foil or use a 6-inch round baking pan. Spray both with cooking spray and place as many slices as can fit without overlapping in the basket.
8. Bake 8 to 12 minutes or until lightly brown. Remove after 2 minutes to a cooling rack.
9. Mix the powdered sugar with enough lemon juice to make a thin icing and drizzle it over each cooking. Let stand until it is set and serve.

NOTE: If you freeze the dough, leave it out for about 10 minutes so the cookies soften up a bit. They may take a little longer to cook if they are still frozen in the middle.

Oatmeal Chocolate Chip Cookies

This dough can also be frozen and cooked at will, which is how I like to do it. This recipe makes 6 dozen cookies and I would be sitting at the air fryer all day if I were to do them all at once. I form the dough in balls and freeze them in freezer bags. When I want a cookie or two, I take 2 balls out of the freezer bag and place them on a plate to defrost about 10 minutes and then pop them in my air fryer. They are really good while they are still warm.

Ingredients:
1 cup butter at room temperature
¾ cup packed brown sugar
¾ cup granulated sugar
2 large eggs
1 teaspoon vanilla
1 ½ cups all-purpose flour
3 cups quick cooking oats
1 3.4-ounce package instant vanilla pudding mix
1 teaspoon salt
1 teaspoon baking soda
2 cups semi-sweet chocolate chips
1 cup chopped nuts

Directions:
1. Place the butter and both sugars in a mixing bowl with an electric mixer and cream well.

255

2. Add the eggs and vanilla and blend in.
3. In a separate bowl combine the flour, oats, instant pudding mix, salt and baking soda and whisk well.
4. At low speed gradually add the flour mixture to the butter mixture until it is all mixed in.
5. Add the chocolate chips and fold in by hand.
6. Preheat the air fryer to 350 degrees for 5 minutes and line the basket with foil or use a baking dish sprayed with cooking spray.
7. Form balls from the dough using a tablespoon, flatten slightly and place 2 inches apart.
8. Cook 8 to 10 minutes or until browned. Let rest 2 minutes and remove to racks.
9. Repeat with the rest of the dough.

Peach Crisp

I grew up on peach crisp and this one is very good. Use either fresh or frozen peach slices and you can even mix it up by using other fruit like apples and berries instead. It makes 4 servings and should be baked in a dish that fits into the air fryer basket or you will have a real mess to clean.

Ingredients:
4 cups sliced peaches (fresh or frozen, thawed and drained)
3 tablespoons sugar and 1 teaspoon sugar, divided
1 tablespoon cinnamon
2 tablespoons and ¼ cup flour, divided

1/3 cup Old Fashion Oats
3 tablespoons unsalted butter at room temperature
3 tablespoons chopped pecans

Directions:
1. Mix the peaches with 3 tablespoons of the sugar and the cinnamon.
2. Spray the baking pan with cooking spray and pour the peach mixture in.
3. Set for 300 degrees F and cook for 10 minutes.
4. Stir the peaches and put in for another 10 minutes.
5. Meanwhile, mix the flour, oats, butter and pecans together well. When time goes off, sprinkle the topping over top of the peaches.
6. Set the temperature to 310 degrees F for 10 minutes and cool for 15 minutes until taking it out of the air fryer and serving.

Peanut Butter and Banana Puffs

These little puffs are like a peanut butter and banana sandwich but fancier. Serve them with vanilla ice cream for a real treat. You use won ton wrappers and it makes 12 treats.

Ingredients:
1 large banana
Water
A splash of lemon juice
12 Won Ton Rappers
½ cup smooth peanut butter
1 to 2 teaspoons coconut oil (you can use vegetable oil too)
Optional add ins:
Chocolate chips
Raisins
Ground cinnamon

Directions:
1. Peel and slice the banana in slices. Place them in enough water to cover with a splash of lemon juice to keep them from turning brown. Set the bowl aside.

257

2. Place a won ton wrapper on a flat surface and remove a banana slice from the water and shake off excess liquid. Place in the won ton wrapper with 1 teaspoon of the peanut butter on top.
3. Brush a little water on the edges of the won ton wrapper.
4. Bring the opposite corners together and squeeze with your fingers. Fold up remaining opposite sides and squeeze with fingers to seal.
5. Spray air fryer basket with cooking spray and place the banana puffs in without overlapping. Do in 2 batches if necessary.
6. Cook at 380 degrees for 6 minutes.

Peanut Butter and Jelly Doughnuts

I often eat peanut butter and jelly toast for breakfast when I am in a hurry or if I crave peanut butter and jelly. These doughnuts make peanut butter and jelly even better. They are crispy on the outside and light and airy on the inside with a peanut butter glaze that will knock your socks off. They do have calories, but not as many as if you were eating doughnuts deep fried in oil. The recipe makes 6 doughnuts and you must cook them in batches. They are heavenly eaten warm. I do make them for in the morning but I also make them as a snack or dessert served with a dollop of whipped cream on the side to dip them in. I have also been known to sprinkle crushed peanuts on top after applying the glaze.

Ingredients for Doughnuts:
2 tablespoons + 1 tablespoon unsalted butter, divided, melted and cooled
1 ¼ cup all-purpose flour
1/3 cup sugar
½ teaspoon baking soda
½ teaspoon baking powder
½ teaspoon salt
1 egg
½ cup buttermilk
1 teaspoon vanilla
Any flavor jelly (not jam – I like strawberry or raspberry)

Ingredients for the Glaze:
½ cup powdered sugar
2 tablespoons peanut butter
2 tablespoons milk
1 pinch sea salt

Directions:
1. Melt 2 tablespoons of butter and let it cool. (If you add it hot, it will cook the egg. It can be warm but if you can't touch it with a finger without getting burned, it is too hot. You don't want it to cool so it solidifies either).
2. In a large bowl, whisk together the flour, sugar, baking soda, baking powder and salt.
3. In a separate bowl, beat the egg, 2 tablespoons melted and cooled butter, buttermilk and vanilla together.
4. Make a well in the center of the flour mixture. Mound it up in the bowl and create a volcano-like crater in the center of the mound. Pour in the egg mixture. Use a fork to start mixing in the dry ingredients into the wet. You knock some dry ingredients into the wet and mix like scrambled eggs but do it gradually until it is all mixed together. Use a large spoon and your hands at the end to get everything well combined.
5. Turn the dough out on a floured surface. The dough will be very sticky so you want to mix the flour in while you work it so it isn't as sticky and becomes very soft and still gooey but doesn't stick to your fingers.
6. Pat the dough out to ¾-inch thickness.
7. Use a 3 ½-inch round cooking cutter to cut out 6 rounds.
8. Melt your remaining 1 tablespoon of butter and brush the tops of each round with it.
9. Cut 2-inch diameter circles of parchment paper and place them on the bottom of the basket of the air fryer. Some air fryers are large and can fit 3 of them in. You are going to place the doughnuts on the parchment so if you have 2 parchment circles, you will put 2 doughnuts in the air fryer. Put the rounds on the parchment paper in the air fryer.
10. Set for 350 degrees F and cook for 11 minutes.

11. Put the jelly in a squeeze bottle (you can use a pastry bag but squeeze bottles work better).
12. Make your glaze while the doughnuts are cooking by whisking the powdered sugar, peanut butter, milk and salt in a bowl. You will have to use some elbow grease to get it to be smooth and fluid.
13. Remove the doughnuts from the air fryer to cool a few minutes until you can handle them and repeat with other rounds.
14. Once you can touch the doughnuts without burning your fingers, fill by inserting the nozzle of the squeeze bottle into the side of the doughnut and squeeze. Don't put too much in. I do one side and then go in on the opposite side and squeeze more in so the jelly is evenly distributed.
15. Place the filled doughnuts on a wire rack over wax paper and drizzle the glaze over each doughnut.
16. Serve warm or cold; warm is better.

Pineapple Cake with Dark Chocolate

This is a decadent cake with tropical flavors and dark chocolate that is supposed to be good for you. I happen to love dark chocolate more than milk, so this was a must try recipe for me. I'm glad I tried it. You must use whole milk instead of 1 or 2 percent or it comes out a little too wet. To get the ¼ cup of pineapple juice, I just drain and press the chunked pineapple into a bowl and if there isn't enough juice to make ¼ cup, I add water or lemon juice. The recipe calls for caster sugar and I would not use anything else. Granulated sugar is too fine. Find caster sugar in the baking section of large grocery stores. You must use a cake pan that fits into the air fryer to make this cake.

Ingredients:
7 tablespoons butter at room temperature
1 cup self-rising flour
½ cup caster sugar
2 cups chunked pineapple
¼ cup pineapple juice
1.75-ounces dark chocolate, grated

2 tablespoons whole milk

1 egg

Directions:

1. Preheat the air fryer to 390 degrees F for 8 minutes. Coat a baking pan that fits into the basket with cooking spray and set aside.
2. Mix the butter and flour in a bowl until it looks like fine bread crumbs. I use a pie cutter or two knives to do this.
3. Add the sugar, pineapple, juice and dark chocolate. Stir until all combined and set that bowl aside.
4. In a small bowl, whisk the milk with the egg.
5. Slowly incorporate the egg mixture into the flour mixture until a batter forms. It should be soft and fluid. Pour into the prepared pan.
6. Set the pan in the air fryer basket and cook for 40 to 45 minutes or until a toothpick inserted into the center of the cake comes out mostly clean. Chocolate may stick to it but that is okay.
7. Let cool about 20 minutes before serving.

Rolled Pie Crust Hand Pies of All Kinds

This is more an explanation on how to make these hand pies than a recipe itself, but these hand pies are folded over, crusty and sweet deliciousness. I use cans of pie filling, but you can also make your own homemade pie filling for strawberry, apple, blueberry, cherry and peach. Add corresponding spices and toppings and you have a real treat you can't find in any grocery store.

Ingredients:
Refrigerated pie crust
canned or homemade pie filling or Nutella, peanut butter, marshmallow fluff or pudding pie fillings.
Spices – cinnamon, nutmeg, cloves, etc.
Toppings = graham crackers, nuts, raw sugars, colored sugars, chocolate or caramel syrups.

Directions:
1. Roll out the pie crust on a lightly floured surface and cut with a 4 ½-inch round cookie cutter. You should get 8 rounds.
2. Fill with Pie filling, nut butters or Nutella, spices of your choice, chocolate chips, nuts. Use 1 heaping tablespoon.
3. Wet the edges of the crust with a little water just to make them moist and fold over the filling into half-moon shapes.
4. Take a fork and press into the edges to seal and crimp
5. Use a sharp knife to put three slashes in the top so the steam can escape while cooking.
6. Preheat the air fryer to 350 degrees F for 5 minutes.
7. Spray the basket with butter flavor cooking spray and place two hand pies in the basket. Spray the pies with the cooking spray. Apply any topping that needs to be cooked including the raw sugar.
8. Cook for 11 minutes – do not turn. The pies should be crusty and brown. Remove and let cool a few minutes.
9. Apply any glaze you might want to use.

NOTES:
- Use Nutella and jelly for Peanut butter and jelly hand pies and place some peanuts or other nuts in the filling for some crunch.
- Place marshmallow fluff in one with some chocolate chips and graham cracker crumbs for S'mores hand pies and then

sprinkle on some graham cracker crumbs on top before cooking.

- Use cherry pie filling with a little cinnamon for cherry hand pies.
- Apple hand pies are great with some cinnamon and nutmeg in them. Make them caramel apple with a drizzle of caramel ice cream topping on top.
- Peach hand pies work with some cinnamon to spice them up.
- Blueberry hand pies don't need anything but the blueberry pie fill in them and maybe a drizzle of powder sugar glaze after they come out of the air fryer.
- Lemon hand pies are made with lemon pie fill or lemon curd with a little lemon zest added. I like lemon and chocolate together so I have been known to add a little bit of semi-sweet chocolate chips with it and drizzle with dark chocolate glaze.
- Pumpkin hand pies are made with pumpkin pie filling, cinnamon, nutmeg, cloves and ginger.

Don't limit yourself; make your own combinations.

Shortbread Wedges

My Celtic grandmother always made shortbread. She put it in a round cake pan and cut it in wedges. Shortbread takes a great deal of butter and more flour than you think can be mixed in. Do not let this surprise you. Because this is a Celtic recipe, it uses Caster sugar which has larger granules than regular sugar. Do not use regular sugar or the shortbread not come out right. Find caster sugar in specialty stores but I have found it in larger grocery stores that stock international foods too. Short bread does not necessarily raise like other cookies do, so there is no leavening agent in the recipe. This makes about 8 to 10 wedges. I like to drizzle mine with a chocolate topping, but you can also leave them plain. This is a converted recipe from English measurements to US measurements, which is why you will see the odd increment of 7/8 cups of butter.

Ingredients:
1 cup all-purpose flour

½ cup Caster sugar

7/8 cup of butter at room temperature (I use unsalted and sprinkle a pinch of sea salt in for a slightly salted flavor)

Directions:

1. Preheat the air fryer to 350 degrees F for 10 minutes.
2. Spray a round cake pan that fits into the air fryer with butter flavored cooking spray and set it aside until needed.
3. In a bowl mix the flour and sugar.
4. Add the butter. Use your hands to take a hand full of the flour and sugar mixture and rub some of the butter in. Use a rubbing motion and let it fall out of your hand. Keep rubbing until the dough is grainy, like fine breadcrumbs but smooth and if you press it together, it solidifies.
5. Pour into the cake pan and press lightly in the bottom. Prick all over with a fork to make little holes in the shortbread and cut into wedges before cooking.
6. Place the pan in the air fryer and cook for 10 minutes. It will depend on how thick the mixture is as to how long it cooks. Mine took about 12 minutes until it was light brown.
7. Let cool a few minutes in the air fryer and remove to a cooling rack.
8. You may have to recut the wedges, but cutting them before cooking avoids breakage.

Sweet Fried Bananas

These yummy sweet bananas are laced with cinnamon and a little bit of sugar, but not much. They are sweet on their own. I don't even make a sauce because they are delicious without it. You cut the banana's in thirds, so it makes 6 pieces of fried banana.

Ingredients:
2 large bananas
¼ cup lemon juice
1/2 cup flour
1 pinch salt
2 eggs, beaten
½ teaspoon cinnamon
1 teaspoon sugar
¾ cup bread crumbs

Directions:
1. Peel and cut each banana into three sections. Place the bananas in lemon juice and roll them around in it. This will prevent them from turning brown. Place them on a baking sheet when done.
2. In one bowl combine the flour and salt.

3. Beat the egg in another bowl.
4. Place the bread crumbs in a separate bowl.
5. Combine the cinnamon and sugar in yet another bowl.
6. Preheat the air fryer to 360 degrees F for 5 minutes. When done, spray with butter flavored cooking spray.
7. Roll one banana section in the flour mixture and dip it in the egg mixture.
8. Place in the breadcrumb mixture and coat the whole section.
9. Place it into the air fryer basket and do the same with 2 more sections.
10. Spray the tops of the bananas with the cooking spray and cook for 4 minutes, shake to move the bananas around and cook another 4 minutes. They should be brown and crispy when done.
11. Immediately remove the banana pieces with tongs and roll them in the cinnamon and sugar and place on a serving plate.
12. Repeat with other three pieces of banana and serve warm. You might want to cool a few minutes before eating.

Sweet Grilled Pineapple

This dessert is great if you don't want something big, just something sweet to end the meal. Use a fresh pineapple because canned pineapple just doesn't hold up well.

Ingredients:
2 teaspoons ground cinnamon
½ cup brown sugar
1 small pineapple, peeled, cored and cut in spears
3 tablespoons melted salted butter

Directions:
1. Combine the cinnamon and sugar in a bowl and set aside.
2. Cut the pineapple and brush each spear with the melted butter.
3. Sprinkle the cinnamon and sugar over, pressing it in to the spear.
4. Spray the air fryer basket with cooking spray and set the spears in in a single layer (you may have two batches).
5. Set for 400 degrees F and cook 10 minutes. Stop half way through to brush with more butter and slightly turn the spears.

NOTE: The first batch should take 10 minutes but because the air fryer is now heated well, the second batch may take less time. They are done when browned and bubbling.

The next chapter goes into cooking frozen or prepared items in the air fryer. You can make onion rings, fries and fish or chicken nuggets that are frozen for a quick meal.

Chapter 12 : Your Favorite Frozen Foods Made Easy

Frozen and packaged food usually do not have instructions for using an air fryer. I have taken several of the most common things you might "reheat" in an air fryer and given you the directions. Onion Rings, fries, breaded chicken and fish and even corn dogs come out great in an air fryer. Remember that not all air fryers are the same. Some might take less or more time, but the temperature is almost always right in the instructions below.

Chicken Breasts

It is possible to take frozen, breaded chicken breasts and cook them in the air fryer without thawing them. They come out nice and crispy. I have done this with plain breaded chicken breasts or frozen chicken Kiev and it works very well.

Ingredients:
4 frozen, breaded chicken breasts (4 usually fit without overlapping)

Directions:
1. Preheat the air fryer to 360 degrees F for 5 minutes
2. Spray the basket with cooking spray.
3. Place the chicken breasts in and cook for 5 minutes, flip and cook another 5 to 6 minutes until toasty and sizzling.

Chicken Nuggets

Chicken nuggets do very well in an air fryer and come out much like they come to you from that certain fast food restaurant that is popular for chicken nuggets. Chicken tenders and strips also can be made the same way.

Ingredients:
10 to 16 frozen chicken nuggets

Directions:
1. Preheat the air fryer to 380 degrees F for 5 minutes.
2. Spray the air fryer basket with cooking spray.
3. Place the nuggets in without overlapping them.
4. Cook 5 minutes, remove basket and shake or turn them over with tongs and cook another 5 minutes. They should be golden brown and slightly sizzle when done.

Chicken Wings

I would not suggest doing chicken wings in the air fryer for a bit party because it just takes too long to make them. You can only put about 4 to 6 wings in and it takes 12 minutes to cook them. But, if you just have a craving for wings and want a few, this is the way to go. The wings can be boneless or bone in and they can be frozen when you put them in the air fryer. You can brush a little barbeque sauce or put salt and pepper on them before you start cooking them if you want.

Ingredients:
4 to 6 chicken wings
Salt and pepper to taste (optional)
Barbeque Sauce (optional)

Directions:
1. Preheat the air fryer to 360 degrees F for 5 minutes.
2. Spray the air fryer basket with cooking spray.
3. Place the wings in the air fryer without overlapping.
4. Sprinkle with salt and pepper or brush with a light coating of barbeque sauce, if desired.
5. Cook 6 minutes, turn (use more salt and pepper or barbeque sauce on the other side) and cook another 6 minutes until done.

Corn Dogs

Frozen corn dogs cook very well in the air fryer and they take very little time. Put them in frozen and I suggest only doing 2 to 3 at a time. Make sure they have wooden sticks and sprits the sticks only with a little water before putting them in. I have had the sticks char a little, but it doesn't happen all the time.

Ingredients:
2 or 3 frozen corn dogs

Directions:
1. Preheat the air fryer to 390 degrees F for 5 minutes.
2. Spray the air fryer basket with cooking spray.
3. Place 2 to 3 frozen corn dogs in the basket.
4. Cook for 7 minutes without turning.

Fish Sticks

Frozen fish sticks or breaded fish fillets come out delightfully crispy on the outside and flaky on the inside. I can get about 6 fish sticks without crowding them and 2 to 3 fillets.

Ingredients:
Frozen fish sticks or fish fillets

Directions:
1. Preheat the air fryer to 360 degrees F for 5 minutes
2. Spray the air fryer basket with cooking spray.
3. Place the sticks or fillets in frozen and cook for 3 minutes, turn and cook another 3 minutes until golden brown. The filets might take 4 minutes, turn and cook another 4 minutes.

French Fries

Frozen French Fries or Potato Wedges are super easy to make in the air fryer. Just make sure you don't over crowd them. They need to be in a single layer when you first cook them. Once all are cooked, dump all of them in and heat for about 2 minutes to make sure they are hot. You can also put them on a baking tray, cover them with foil and put them in the oven at the lowest setting (usually 200 or 250 degrees F) to keep them warm.

Ingredients:

Frozen French Fries or Potato Wedges

Directions:
1. Preheat the air fryer to 380 degrees F for fries and 400 degrees F for wedges for 5 minutes.
2. Spray the air fryer basket with cooking spray.
3. Place fries or wedges in a single layer.
4. Cook 10 minutes for thin fries, 12 minutes for fatter fries and 14 minutes for wedges. Always pause half way through and shake the basket and complete the cooking.

Hamburgers

Many people purchase frozen hamburgers because they are very economical. These can be made in an air fryer and they come out nicely. Use a pan inside the air fryer basket, like a 6-inch round cake pan that has been sprayed with cooking spray. There will be a little grease involved just because it is a hamburger. If you take it out right after it is done cooking and place the patty on a paper towel covered plate, you will not get all the grease on the burger. Some air fryers have grill pans with raised ripples that deflect any grease away from the food.

Ingredients:
1 hamburger patty, 2 if they fit without overlapping

Directions:
1. Preheat the air fryer to 360 degrees F for 5 minutes.
2. Spray the pan with cooking spray and set one or two patties in.
3. Cook for 7 minutes, flip the patties over and cook another 6 to 7 minutes.

Jalapeno Poppers

Homemade poppers are much better than frozen, but if you are in a pinch for a light appetizer the frozen types will come out very nicely in the air fryer.

Ingredients:
Box of Jalapeno Poppers

Directions:
1. Set the air fryer to 400 degrees F and preheat for 5 minutes.
2. Spray the basket of the air fryer with cooking spray.
3. Place as many poppers as can fit in the bottom of the basket
4. Cook for 10 minutes. Do not shake or turn midway, just let them go.

Mozzarella Sticks

Mozzarella sticks are a favorite appetizer, but kids like them after school and it is so simple to throw a few in the air fryer for a few minutes and serve.

Ingredients:
1. Preheat the air fryer to 400 degrees F for 5 minutes
2. Spray the air fryer basket with cooking spray.
3. Place as many mozzarella sticks as will fit in the bottom of the basket.
4. Cook 10 minutes without shaking or turning midway.
5. Serve with marinara sauce or ranch dressing.

Onion Rings

Making homemade onion rings is messy. Using frozen ones can save you time and mess although they aren't near as good. They work in a pinch though.

Ingredients:
Frozen Onion Rings

Directions:
1. Preheat the air fryer to 360 degrees F for 5 minutes.
2. Spray the air fryer basket with cooking spray.
3. Place about 8 to 10 rings in. They are going to overlap because they are round, but try not to overlap too many.

4. Cook 4 minutes, turn the onion rings with rubber tipped tongs and put in another 3 minutes.
5. Serve with dipping sauce.

Pierogi

Cooking pierogi in the air fryer is more like having deep fried pierogi. They come out crusty on the outside and soft on the inside. Use a pan inside the air fryer basket because you will be brushing them with melted butter or buffalo sauce and that makes a mess in the basket.

Ingredients:
1 box frozen pierogis
Buffalo Sauce or Melted butter
Blue Cheese Dressing or Sour Cream

Directions:
1. Preheat the air fryer to 360 for 5 minutes
2. Spray the pan that goes in the air fryer basket with cooking spray and set it in.
3. Place about 6 perogies in the pan and cook for 6 minutes.
4. Brush the tops of the pierogi with a light coating of buffalo sauce or melted butter.
5. Put them back in to cook 2 more minutes.
6. Serve with blue cheese dressing or sour cream.

Pizza

I can fit a 6 to 4=inch pizza in my air fryer. I put it right in the air fryer basket and cook it. Just loosen the edges when done and pour it out onto a paper plate. You can also do frozen slices of pizza. The pizza crust comes out nice a crispy.

Ingredients:
A frozen pizza that fits in the air fryer basket
Extra Parmesan and/or Mozzarella cheese

Directions:

1. Preheat the air fryer to 400 degrees F for 4 minutes.
2. Spray cooking spray in the air fryer basket.
3. Set pizza in basket and cook for 10 minutes.
4. If pizza is not brown and bubbly, set for 5 more minutes.
5. Sprinkle with parmesan and/or mozzarella and put in 1 more minute.

Pizza rolls

Pizza rolls are easy to make in the air fryer and they come out better than if you made them in the oven.

Ingredients:
Pizza Rolls

Directions
1. Preheat the air fryer to 380 degrees F for 5 minutes.
2. Spray the air fryer basket with cooking spray.
3. Place as many pizza rolls in the basket in one layer. Try not to overlap. If you want to do more, do two batches.
4. Cook 4 minutes, shake the basket to turn the pizza rolls about, cook another 3 minutes and serve.

Taquitos

Frozen taquitos are a time saver and they might not be as delicious as those you make yourself, but if you are in a hurry, they are not too bad. Dip them in salsa/and or sour cream and enjoy.

Ingredients:
Frozen taquitos

Directions:
1. Preheat the air fryer to 400 degrees F for 4 minutes.
2. Spray the air fryer basket with cooking spray.
3. Place as many taquitos in as can fit in the basket without overlapping.

4. Cook 5 minutes, shake the basket and cook another 3 minutes.

Tater Tots

Tater tots are perfect for the air fryer. They come out delightfully crisp and delicious. Do not over crowd the basket or they will not crisp up. Do only as many as can fit in the bottom without overlapping and that might mean you have to do more than one batch.

Ingredients:
Frozen tater tots

Directions:
Preheat air fryer to 400 degrees F for 4 minutes
1. Spray the air fryer basket with cooking spray and spray again for each batch.
2. Pour in enough tater tots to cover the bottom of the basket without overlapping.
3. Cook for 5 minutes, shake the basket and cook another 5 minutes.

Conclusion

You are now well on your way to eating great with the 200 recipes in this book. Be sure to experiment with your favorite recipes and make them your own. Try making two or three new recipes each week, replacing unhealthier versions with the ones in this book. I think you will find that you will love all the possibilities that your Air Fryer provides you. Enjoy the ease of creating your favorite meals and trying out new recipes that your friends and family are sure to love! Most of all, have some fun cooking and start eating like royalty!

I wish you great health and delicious meals on your life's journey!

Thanks for reading.

If this book has helped you or someone you know then I invite you to leave a nice review right now. **It would be greatly appreciated!**

My Other Books

For more great books simply visit my author page or type my name into the Kindle Store or Books search bar: **Susan Hollister**

Author Page

USA: https://www.amazon.com/author/susanhollister

UK: http://amzn.to/2qiEzA9

Thanks and Enjoy!